# INVADING THE DARKNESS

*Power Evangelism Training 101*

May the Lord
WRAP His Presence
around you.

Steve P___

**Steve Porter**

*This book is dedicated to **Alyssa and Britney Porter**.*

*You both are world shakers and history makers for Jesus Christ... Born **"For Such a Time as This"**!*

**and**

*To **Chris Branson***

*You carry a Generational Mantle for Healing and Souls , and your legacy is being written as we speak. Embrace your purpose and watch your destiny beautifully unfold.*

'Now get up and stand on your feet. I have appeared to you to appoint you as a servant and as a witness of what you have seen and will see of me.

I will rescue you from your own people and from the Gentiles. I am sending you to them

 to open their eyes and turn them from darkness to light, and from the power of Satan to God, so that they may receive forgiveness of sins and a place among those who are sanctified by faith in me.'

**Acts 26:16-18**

# ACKNOWLEDGEMENTS

Special Thanks to Marie Lawson my editor, writer and researcher. Some of this book was written in the 90's and sat on a shelf until Marie dusted it off, polished it up and then added so much more to it! Thank you!

# TABLE OF CONTENTS

# SECTION 1
## The Harvest is Great

# AVAILABILITY

It doesn't take a rocket scientist to figure out that we live in a pretty messed-up world. Our values have gone to pot. The morals of this country have greatly deteriorated with the breakdown of the family. Negative role models are replacing real heroes to our children. America's cities are virtual battlegrounds of chaos. People are living in constant fear. Many teens go to school afraid for their very lives! Our children today, see things unheard of a few short years ago. Killing sprees in the nation's schools are being reported more and more frequently by the news media. Yet, God is in the midst of this out-of-control world. Perhaps you're wondering, "Where do I fit in all this?" The answer is the same as it has been in every age – look to God, make Him the Lord of your life. Let Him fix the circumstances. God wants to place within you a burden to make a difference in all this insanity – God wants to use you! You may think, "How can I make a difference. I'm not qualified and I'm only one person. What could I do?"

**I believe God is saying to you, my child, "I will use you and anyone who will make themselves available to me!"**

# THE BURDEN

When I first graduated from Bible school I was full of enthusiasm, but lacked confidence. I wanted to win the world over for Jesus, but fear held me back. I was afraid to open my mouth and let the truth come out. One night the Lord spoke to my heart to go down to a local park and spread the Gospel. I thought to myself, *"How in the world am I going to do that."* I felt intimidated by teenagers. Though I had no desire, I knew what God had said. For days I wrestled with God's clear command, until finally I gave in and told the Lord I would go. Two things I asked of the Lord, that He would give me boldness and a genuine desire to reach out to teens. To my surprise that's just what he did. Soon, a burden for the teens in my town kept me awake at night. I knew that no matter what happened as a result, I had to go to that park. My prayers became more and more fervent, and I felt as if God had set me on fire. I went to that park a changed man. To my amazement, I had a boldness I never experienced before. I began to preach to teens who were on drugs and came from dysfunctional families. Even as I spoke, young people ran over and surrounded me. They couldn't believe that someone could be "into Jesus" that much. I just stood there in shock because I knew my words were not my own. Twelve teens were saved in two days. I handed out New Testaments, assigned Bible reading, and brought some of the teens to church. This was the beginning of my ministry. That summer, the Lord set me free from fear and I led many to Christ. It was such a miracle to me that God would use someone so afraid and unsure of himself. I pray that all those souls I led to the Lord are still following God. I do know many seeds were planted in their hearts that summer.

# ABILITY/ AVAILABILITY

There's nothing particularly special about me. What revolutionized me and eventually changed those around me – was my prayer. I asked the Lord for a desire, and made myself available to Him. My Friend if you will do the same, He'll use you too. Like me, you may not feel capable, **<u>but with Christ you can do all things!</u>**

**It's not your ability, but your availability that counts.**

It doesn't matter how talented you are, or how much you know. What really matters is that you have a heart for God and a desire to be used.

# DEPENDENCE

When I took my second missionary trip to India at the age of 18 by all human standards it was a flop. I remember the first time I got up to speak to the "Nationals". I asked my leader how long my sermon should be. He said, "Oh, about 30 minutes." I about fainted right there on the spot. As I opened my mouth to speak, nothing would come out except an empty promise to tell my country about them when I returned home. I managed to tell a story I once read, but I knew I was not effective. All my words toppled to the ground. My team members and my leaders were all disappointed in me. I heard my name mentioned in many conversations and knew the things they said were not positive. To make matters worse, even the pastors of the Indian church were talking. I felt humiliated and of no use whatsoever that summer. Little did I know that God was teaching me a powerful lesson.

When I was in Bible school I took another trip, this time to Jamaica. When I got up to preach I felt totally different, almost as if I were on fire. I began to preach, as I never had before. Instead of my words falling to the ground, the Lord anointed me. I saw nearly 100 people come to Christ during my two weeks there. I recall one night after I gave the invitation to come forward to receive salvation, 25 came to the altar to accept Christ. I just stood at the pulpit and marveled. I couldn't believe it; this was so different from India. The Lord spoke to me sometime later. He said:

**"Steve do you remember India? That was your ability. Do you remember Jamaica? That was my ability and anointing placed in you."**

# ANOINTING

You see, it 's not your talent or ability that will win the lost and make a difference. This can be accomplished only through God, placing within you <u>His</u> anointing. Put your mind at rest, and realize God will speak through you as you ask Him. Do not focus on your **weakness** or **lack of ability**, but on Jesus who <u>will strengthen you.</u>

**Phil. 4:13 –" I can do everything through Him who gives me strength." (KJV)**

Pray for God's anointing daily, and He will place within you all you need. Make yourself available to the Lord, and <u>stand back and see what God will do through you!</u>

# FROM SHEPHERD BOY TO KING

I am reminded of the story of David. David was just a shepherd boy. His job was to take care of the sheep which, by earthly standards, was an insignificant task. One day the prophet Samuel came to the house of Jesse and told him He was sent to anoint one of his sons to be King. Jesse brought all of his sons together for this great event; all except David. After all he reasoned, why would God want a shepherd boy? Each son passed before Samuel. A son who was considered important, muscular and looking the part of a king, went before Samuel. He was rejected. Another son, both intelligent and eloquent, stood before the prophet Samuel. Surely, he would be <u>the one.</u> But, this son was also dismissed. In turn, all Jesse's other sons were likewise rejected. When Samuel asked if there was anyone left, I'm sure they all thought, "Yes, only David, but he's out with the sheep." "Bring him to me " said Samuel. When David went before the prophet, he appeared to be <u>a rugged, unqualified youth.</u> Someone you would never think would be a king.

**After all, why would God choose a shepherd boy to be king?**

But praise our God, the scriptures tell us God delights in choosing the person of low estate – the one the world least expects – to perform His will and purposes. When **David** stood before Samuel, to everyone's amazement, it was he whom Samuel anointed – **King!**

**Why was David chosen King?** Was it for his strength? Was it for his intelligence? Was it for his wisdom? Was it for his good looks? It was evident none of these things fulfilled the criteria. **David was chosen because of his heart.**

**God chooses us today, based upon our heart, not our qualifications. <u>God rarely calls the qualified, He qualifies the called!</u>**

The only qualification David had was his earnest, heartfelt de-

7

sire to serve God. God **prepared** David to be King **after** he was anointed. God will also prepare you to accomplish the task he has set for you. I believe that task, my friend, is to make a difference in this world. <u>God always looks straight to the heart to see if there is one who will make himself available to Him</u>. Will you be that one?

# BOLDNESS

How many people do you pass in the hallways of your school <u>who may be going to **Hell**</u>? We can no longer wait until they hear a preacher, we must reach them ourselves. You can reach people that "the preacher" will never reach. People reaching people is the best way to go. You can relate to your friends in a way that no one else can.

**God has placed you in your circle of influence so that you may be His mouthpiece.**

Don't let your friends go to Hell because you are <u>ashamed.</u>

**Paul said "For I am not ashamed of the gospel: for it is the power of God unto salvation to every one that believes." (Rom. 1:16)**

<u>The gospel of Christ is power</u>. It has meat. It has strength. It is an awesome Word! You can take that powerful, awesome word to your city. <u>You</u> can make a difference in someone's life.

<u>Even if you can only influence one precious soul before you die, it is still worthwhile sharing Christ</u>. I believe God wants to use you much more than that, but if just one person goes to Heaven because of you, it is still a soul **saved** from eternal separation from God. Instead of burning in Hell for all of eternity, that person can enjoy Heaven because you decided to make a difference in your world. You were willing to make yourself available to God and be bold.

I remember when I was in Jamaica, I had just preached and given the altar call. One lone Jamaican boy about eight years old came to the altar. No one else responded to the invitation. My heart went out to Him. He came with tears in his eyes, crying out to God for forgiveness. He wept and wept as he cried out to God to save him. And he was gloriously saved. The only person that day, who desired the Christ of Calvary, was that eight-year old boy. But, I would have still gone to Jamaica, just for him. The joy I experienced will never be forgotten. Reaching just one soul for Him will place within you a real desire for the lost – and an incomparable joy.

If you don't have a burden for the lost, ask God to give you one. I didn't have a burden for those teens at the park, until God placed them on my heart. He's willing to place a burning burden in **you,** if He knows you will respond. Make up your mind to make yourself available no matter what. You'll be surprised at what God will lay upon your heart. But, He doesn't expect you to carry that burden by yourself. He'll be right alongside.

**We should never run from God, but respond to Him in <u>obedience</u>.**

If you have a God-given burden, He alone will equip you with everything you need to fulfill it. Go forth with boldness, because God will enable you.

We are called to be <u>ambassadors of Christ,</u> to tell people of His <u>ministry of reconciliation</u>. There is a great responsibility on the Christian today. It's very important to reach out to our lost and hurting world, as never before. First, we need to pray for boldness and get the message of God in our hearts, then go out and share the Gospel in a way that's simple for all to understand. The presentation of the Gospel should never be complex or difficult to understand. God will help you by putting the words into your mouth **after** He has put them into your heart. In **Jeremiah 1**, the Lord speaks of putting the words into our mouths because He has ordained us. The Lord is speaking to Jeremiah here, but we can make practical use of it and apply it to our lives.

People may not always accept us, nevertheless, we must at least tell them.

**Often the seed you plant in someone's life will be watered in years to come. But eventually, that seed will reap a harvest.**

<u>Don't be discouraged if people don't respond to you</u>. Leave the results in God's hands. You may never know the outcome, but be of good cheer, **a seed has been planted!**

One day, I was sitting in Taco Bell and the Lord spoke to me and told me to go up to a certain young man and tell him Jesus cares for him. I said, "Lord, is that really you?" The burden continued to burn within me and I knew what I had to do. I thought to myself, *"This guy will think I'm crazy."* I <u>ignored </u>my thoughts and approached him with a smile. "You may think I'm crazy, but God told me to come to you and tell you He cares about you." He just looked at me somewhat startled and said, "Oh, ok, thank you." I smiled and walked out the door. I don't know what happened afterward, but I do know <u>a seed was planted</u>. I had to leave the results in God's hands. I rejoiced that I had obeyed the Lord.

**<u>It is more important to obey God than to see results</u>.**

**Let God take care of the details. You just obey his voice. Then there are special times when God allows <u>you</u> to reap a harvest.**

The story is told of D. L. Moody, perhaps the greatest personal soul winner of his day, where he made it a practice of his life to speak to men on the streetcars. Speaking to a man on a Detroit streetcar, he asked him the question, "Are you a Christian?" The man answered, "No sir, but I wish I were." D. L. Moody without hesitation led the man to Christ. You see God may allow you to win someone to Christ right there on the spot like D. L. Moody, or you may just sow a seed. No matter what the outcome, **<u>DO NOT BE DISCOURAGED</u>**! I will speak about more powerful soul winners later on in this training book.

I like the compelling words of Keith Green. He said,

**"You have to be called to stay, because we are already called to go."**

We can no longer excuse ourselves by saying "sharing the Gospel is not my ministry." Jesus declares we are all to go and share the good news.

There's a world out there full of hurting people. Increasingly, only a small fraction of professed Christians ever make any personal effort to share Jesus, or to help a hurting person. Comparatively fewer of the most earnest people see any numbers saved, except during the short period of the year when evangelistic services are held. If you are a young person, **you** are the leaders of tomorrow. Don't let your generation go to Hell while you stand there and watch. **Stand up! Be bold! You can turn your generation upside down for Christ**. If you are older I give you this same charge! In these last days, God is raising up an army of bold trail blazers who will rise up and proclaim that Jesus is Lord. You can be in this army, dear one ,**if** you will make yourself available.

# BE A LIGHT

One of the biggest hindrances to sharing faith is that many feel they must be **perfect** before they can tell others the good news. You can't wait until you're a perfect saint to go out and share Christ. You'll never be perfect in the sight of God on this side of Heaven. Having said that, it is still true that in order for us to offer the world "something better", our lives must reflect that "better" ideal.

**You can't deliberately live in sin and rebellion and expect God to use you.**

Our Christian walk must be <u>different</u> from the world. You may make some mistakes, but if you're really committed to God – if you give your life unreservedly over to Him – you can be used of God.

Our own righteousness, as described by the prophet Isaiah (64:4) **"is as filthy rags."** What should we do? In sincere repentance we ask forgiveness for our sin and move on, striving with the Lord's help, to become what He wants us to be. And we keep right on reaching out to others.

# JESUS DECLARES
# YOU ARE A LIGHT!

**"You are the light for the whole world. A city built on top of a hill <u>cannot be hidden</u>, and no one would light a lamp and put it under a clay pot. A lamp is placed on a lamp-stand, where it can give light to everyone in the house. <u>Make your light shine so that others will see the good that you do and will praise your Father in heaven</u>."** Matthew 54-16.

Our very dark world desperately needs a light. You and I can be that light. Do you, precious one, shine bright as a light? Do people see something different about you? <u>People should know we're saved without us telling them.</u> No one has to tell you when the sun is shining, the same should be true in our Christian lives. If you're a Christian and walk after the light, you too should be shining. We are called to be **lighthouses** for Jesus. Do you shine that all may see your good works? Do your friends see that light and recognize you as a Christian? Or do you hide your light? In **Matthew 5** Jesus tells us to shine and not cover our candle. Do you act one way at church and another way at work or school? This is hiding your candle. Remember if you hide your light because you're ashamed of Jesus now on Earth, He will be ashamed of you before the Father in heaven,

**"If you are ashamed of me and my message, the Son of Man will be ashamed of you when he comes in his glory and in the glory of his Father and the holy angels."** Luke 9:26

I remember many years ago when I started a new job after Bible school. I worked as a waiter at Ponderosa Steak House for extra money. The manager knew I was a pastor. My first day was one of great temptation. I noticed some very attractive girls with whom I'd be working, and the thought came to me that if I kept my mouth shut about being a preacher I might get a date. I was also afraid they'd make fun of me and think I was weird. I wasn't married yet and didn't even have a girl friend. My loneliness was sometimes overwhelming. But, I had to decide if I was going to hide my candle, or let it shine brightly.

**My fellow workers could be going to Hell and here I am considering hiding my light. No way!!!**

After some serious thought, I decided I would not deny my Father by hiding my light. Why risk everything for temporary approval? I couldn't risk jeopardizing eternal souls just for companionship, for fleeting pleasure. They needed Jesus!

I had to make myself available to the Lord. Soon everyone found out I was a preacher. After some time they began to respect who I was, and I had the opportunity of sharing my faith with them. I know without a doubt I was a light in that place and a blessing, and at the same time I gained a lot spiritually. The Lord gave me a look at reality, and I'll never be the same. I praise God I didn't hide my light. I would have missed so much.

If you're no different from the world, if your light doesn't shine, the world will not want the Jesus you preach. They'll see no difference between your Jesus and their own fabricated god. The world is looking for answers. The answers they seek are to be found in Jesus, the eternal Light.

**God's light exposes their darkness and reveals their need for Him.**

Precious one, you can invade the darkness with God's light shining from you. You can be a carrier of God's light. You may ask, Steve how can I shine? I'm a Christian, but my light doesn't shine very brightly. That's a very good question. If you want your light to shine brighter you must go to the **Source** of all light.

15

**Spending time in prayer increases your light. The more you hang out with Jesus the more He will rub off on you.**

If you spend only two minutes a day in prayer, don't expect to be a lighthouse, but rather a nightlight at best. If you, precious one, begin to diligently spend time in prayer, and in study of His Word, you will be changed. People will know there's something different about you. They'll recognize your light. Start today by spending quality time with the Lord and you will shine with an obvious brightness. **You** will be able to make a difference in this crazy mixed up world.

# GOD'S PLAN

One morning during a church service I was attending, the Holy Spirit spoke to my heart. He brought me to the book of <u>Jeremiah, chapter 1</u> and began teaching me. Over the years this passage has remained fresh in my spirit. In these scriptures the Lord is speaking to Jeremiah.

Verse 5 **"Before I formed thee in the belly I knew thee: and before you came forth out of the womb I sanctified you, and I ordained you a prophet unto the nations. Then said I, Ah, Lord God! Behold, I cannot speak: for I am a child. But the Lord said unto me, <u>Behold, I have put my words in your mouth</u>. See, I have this day set you over the nations and over the kingdoms, to root out, and to pull down, and destroy, and throw down, to build, and to plant."** Jeremiah 5-10

Since the Lord gave me this passage, my life has not been the same. Do you realize God knew you would be born <u>before</u> the foundations of the world? You're very special to Him. Just ponder this fact for a moment. You are <u>special</u> to the **Creator** of the universe. There may be billions of people on this planet, yet God thinks <u>you're</u> special.

**Even when you were in the womb of your mother God had a plan for your life.**

God wants to reveal His plan to you. Realize deep down – God is not passing you over; He is not ignoring you. God has a very special plan for your life that only you can fulfill. Satan would try to convince you that you don't count, that God could never use you. Don't buy that lie, it's straight from hell. You must throw out these ideas if you're ever to be used of God. Satan may keep up a running dialogue, speaking discouragement to your mind. **Don't listen!** Satan's always been a liar. You are very important to the

Lord, and when you <u>believe</u> this you will go places.

I'm not suggesting everyone is called to be a pastor, but everyone **is** called to reach out to a dying world headed for hell. God's plan is that we direct the lost from the wide road leading to death to the narrow road that leads to life. **(Matthew 7:13)** Remember, only you can fulfill your specific calling in the unique way that God has given you.

<u>In verse six</u> Jeremiah tells the Lord he's just a child. In other words Jeremiah was letting the Lord know how inadequate he felt for his calling. The thing you must realize is God already knows your limitations. Jeremiah thought he should remind God. God responds to Jeremiah by telling him not to be down on himself, but that the Lord would <u>fill his mouth and send him out</u>. This brings me great joy because I realize God knows my inadequacy very well, and **He** will be faithful to **empower** me to do His will for my life. We are only responsible to obey God in moving out. The Lord will take care of the details. Again, to quote Keith Green in one of his songs:

**"Give the Lord your best, pray that it's blessed, and God will take care of the rest."**

Will you trust God, precious one, to touch your life as He did Jeremiah? God will also enable <u>you</u> to do His will. God is no respecter of persons. What He did for Jeremiah He'll do for you! That day in church, this revelation forever changed me. My prayer for you today is that you too will know you are special to God. I pray that you would know your calling and begin to move out in faith. God will empower you with His boldness and anointing to fulfill His purpose. In the areas you lack, God will move supernaturally on your behalf. God wants to uses you, regardless of your calling. If you're called to be a preacher or a Burger King cook, God will use you to lead others to the way of truth and life. Allow God to perform a miracle in your life as He did for Jeremiah. **Remember God rarely calls the qualified, He <u>qualifies</u> the called.**

# COMPARING

I believe God desires to transform people from the role of spectator to the work of participant, in winning our world for Jesus. God desires to take you off the sidelines and make you effective in your world. Do you want to become a Christian of action? You can! Never settle for just talking about "taking over the world." Don't just watch others do it, but allow God to empower you to be all you can be for Christ. God has a plan only you can fulfill. **He has a special gifting for you!** Don't compare yourself with others. <u>Remember God has a special place just for you.</u>

Looking back at myself at age 19, when God first called me into the ministry, I knew the Lord had a plan for my life. I desired to be used of God, but felt so inadequate. My problem was every time I heard someone preach I always compared myself to them. I would say things like "I could never make my words flow like that", or "they're so talented and they look so good up there". Sometimes I felt I would burst if I sat in another service. I had such an intense desire to share Christ, but my doubts held me back. Finally, through a lot of inner struggle, I came to the end of myself. The Lord began to show me I had a specific calling and no one else could fulfill it. I had to stop comparing myself to others and start focusing on Him. I don't have to preach like someone else, just be myself. <u>God only expects us to be ourselves.</u>

**The world doesn't need clones. We need people who will reach out in a fresh new way.**

God desires you to be all you can be for Him. He requires us to do our best, and then He promises to do the rest. When you compare yourself with others you will always feel you fall short of who they are. Don't allow yourself to be cheated out of what God has for you because of futile comparison. **You will only end up a spectator Christian.**

God desires to take you off the sidelines. He desires for you to be all you can be for Christ in your own **unique** way. Put your complete trust in God because with Him we can do all things.

# GOD'S STRENGTH

**"But they that wait upon the Lord shall renew their strength: they shall mount up with wings as eagles: they shall run, and not be weary: and they shall walk and not faint."** (Isaiah 40:31 KJV)

It is of greatest importance that you be filled with Gods strength before you "invade the darkness for Jesus Christ." If you're to win the world for Jesus, you must tap into the strength only God can supply. Without it you won't survive. **Satan will come to blast you with His discouragement and doubt and your own strength won't be enough to fight Him off**. It's so easy to become weary when results aren't what you hoped for. You may be tempted to give up and say "Forget it, I'm not really making any difference." It's easy to throw in the towel when you don't have His strength to sustain you. A car can't run without fuel, it will gradually slow down and finally stop. In the same manner, we can't press on without fueling our spirits. Understand this – Christ is the source of all strength. We must go to Him daily for our "gasoline", through prayer and reading His word.

**No time spent fueling up in His presence is wasted time.**

Every moment spent in prayer will fill your spiritual tank more and more. Satan will come to you. He'll tell you that you're wasting your time. He'll whisper in your ear that nothing is happening. Every moment you spend in God's presence gives you more "gas" empowering you to finish the task.

**If Satan can stop you from praying, he has successfully stopped the inflow of your strength and power.**

Don't let Satan win the battle, even when you don't see results right away. Let me say this again, sometimes God doesn't allow you to see the results immediately. He wants you to grow in perseverance, faith, and strength. I remind you there are times we only plant the seeds and others reap the harvest. Be faithful and you will be rewarded, if not here, then someday in heaven.

Satan loves to convince us we'll fall flat on our face and look like a fool. He'll tell you that you're a "nobody" lacking what it takes for your calling. But remember, these satanic attacks leave out the power of God. With God we can do all things! **If we believe the lie of Satan we will be sapped of our strength.** You will no longer come to the Lord as your source, but instead you'll drown in your tears of self -pity. You'll expect failure before you even start out. The flow of God's strength will not be yours because you are looking in the mirror, instead of heavenward. Believe you're a child of God and you and Jesus can win the world!

**In** Philippians 4:13 **it says, "I can do all things through Christ which strengthens me."**

The key here is "through Christ," Not through you, through Him! Even Jesus, while on this earth, constantly spent time alone with His father. Jesus needed to go to Him for His strength and encouragement. (Mark 1:35; Luke 5:16; John 6:15; Luke 22:39-44)

"They that wait upon the Lord shall renew their strength." The key is to wait. Go to God anticipating that He is filling you, even when you don't feel it. Begin by praying whatever is on your heart to God, then become real quiet and listen. The Holy Spirit may begin to move upon you. Don't be afraid, but realize He is filling you. When you sit in quietness and begin "waiting on Him" your focus will change to Jesus instead of yourself. This puts you in a place where you can receive from God. The term "to renew" is very expressive. To renew strength really means to exchange strength. It is important we rid ourselves of self-strength so that God may clothe us with His strength. Being quiet before God with our hearts directed toward Him accomplishes this very thing. Waiting on God is not just folding your arms and letting God know you're waiting around for Him. Rather you're in an active listening mode with an expectant attitude, ready to hear from God and receive His necessary strength. The exchange will take place and you'll be clothed with all you need to invade the darkness of the enemy. This is exciting, precious one, because through your "waiting" you receive all you need – by the exchange of your clothes for His.

# PERSECUTION

Another very important thing to remember is when you begin to be a light and move out in boldness, persecution is inevitable. Satan today, as in the past, hates Jesus and all of His creation. When we're walking in a manner that portrays Jesus Christ, you can bet that obstacles, as well as persecution from the world will come. The world persecutes the Christian without even realizing that the enemy, Satan, is using them as a puppet. Because the ordinary world doesn't know Jesus, they walk around in complete blindness and bitterness toward anything that is pure. Not all the world is unkind and cruel toward Christians, however you will always face a certain amount of persecution.

The astonishing aspect of persecution is the Lord commands we love and pray for our persecutors. This doesn't mean you have to like what they do, but we're to love them and be exceedingly glad, even in our persecution. (Matthew 5:12). The question which comes to mind is how can you be glad when persecution comes? I feel the answer to that question is found in Matthew 5:12:

**"Rejoice, and be exceeding glad: <u>for great is your reward</u> in heaven: for so persecuted they the prophets which were before you"**

When you give up popularity and your own personal ego for the Lord, Jesus will bless you. Every time someone laughs at you, or picks on you, and you love them anyway, God will take notice of this and reward you. You may never see your reward in this lifetime, but in eternity you will be blessed.

America has not experienced persecution like many other nations of this world do. I believe there's coming a day when we too may have to face much adversity. What will you do? Will you stand up for God and be bold even if it costs you your life? Lets examine some men of the past and see how they reacted to persecution.

**In Acts chapter 6 and 7,** we can read the account of Stephen's life. Stephen was chief of seven deacons. He straightened out the complaints in the Jerusalem church. Stephen wasn't a man to "go with the flow." He would boldly denounce the local worship along with the Jewish customs belonging to it. He stood up for what was right.

These Hellenistic Jews were jealous of him, because they were no match for Stephen in an argument. As a result, they hired false witnesses and brought Stephen before the same Sanhedrin who crucified Christ. Standing before the Council, he then had a chance to address the Sanhedrin in his own defense. This part of the story is what really ministers to me. Stephen had a chance to completely deny Christ and save his life. Or he could stand up for Jesus and lose his life. I believe Stephen didn't even have to think about it. He immediately chose his Lord – **Jesus.** We can see in his address before the Council, that Stephen strongly rebuked them for their murder of Jesus, and proclaimed Jesus as the Christ, the Son of God.

Acts 7:51-53- **"You stubborn and hardheaded people! You are always fighting against the Holy Spirit, just as your ancestors did. Is there one prophet that your ancestors didn't mistreat? They killed the prophets who told about the coming of the One Who Obeys God. And now you have turned against him and killed him. Angels gave you God's Law but you still don't obey it."**

When the judges heard this, they could listen no longer. They rushed upon him eagerly dragging him out of the city to the place of his execution and stoned him to death. Read about how Stephen died in the 7th chapter of Acts.

Paul, the first apostle to the Gentiles, watched as stones fell upon Stephen. Stephen, all the while, called upon Jesus whom he saw in the Heavens, and repeated those same words Jesus said on the cross:

**"Receive my Spirit, and lay not this sin to their charge." (Acts 7: 59-60- As Stephen was being stoned to death, he called out, "Lord Jesus welcome me!" He knelt down and shouted, "Lord do not blame them for what they have done." Then he died.)**

God's glory was upon Stephen as he died; he was without resentment towards his contemptible murderers. Stephen gave up his life and would not denounce Jesus. If he would have denied him, he probably would have been spared. Instead, he stood firmly in what he strongly believed and gave up his life for the King of kings.

Another good example of a man who actually practiced loving his enemies in time of persecution, and for whom I have great respect, is a bishop of Antioch named Ignatius, who was a student of the Apostle John. He was martyred to Rome A.D. 110. Ignatius was put on trial and sentenced to be thrown to the wild beasts. On his way to his death, he begged the Roman Christians not to procure his pardon. Ignatius longed to give up his life for the Lord. He said some very compelling words. **"May the wild beast be eager to rush upon me. If they be unwilling I will compel them, come crowd of wild beasts, come tearing and mangling, wracking of bones and breaking of limbs; come cruel tortures of the devil only let me attain unto Christ."** I know this statement is graphic, but it shows us what a man totally sold out to God can do. I marvel at the extraordinary love for Christ Ignatius exhibited and his bravery in the face of such extreme persecution.

Polcarp made these compelling comments when the governor pleaded with him to deny Christ or be thrown to the beasts, **"<u>Bring the beasts</u>."** When the governor said he would have him burned at the stake, Polycarp replies, **"<u>You try to frighten me with fire that burns for an hour, and yet forget the fire of hell that never goes out.</u>"** Polycarp too was a man filled with boldness. At his stake he prays that his death would be an acceptable sacrifice.

These are examples of men whose light was bright and who were very bold in their day. They looked upon persecution as a blessing, not a curse. Precious one, are you willing to love your enemies and those who persecute you, even if it costs you your life someday? Can you forgive and begin to pray for those who hurt you? Remember the best kind of revenge is prayer!

Today, as Americans, we can be very thankful we're not yet faced with extreme persecution. The next time we face persecution for our faith, we can remind ourselves of Stephen, Ignatius, Polycarp. This should bring forth a fresh gratitude in our hearts. We will realize that we're not the only ones who have faced persecution, but countless others have paid an even greater price.

One martyr who has touched so many hearts, is the girl from Columbine High School who, when asked by her attackers if she believed in God replied, "Yes I believe in God " She then was shot to her death. I picture her standing before God as He reaches out to touch her saying, "Well done my faithful servant. Enter into my glory."

# THE SHADRACH, MESHACH, AND ABEDNEGO GENERATION

God, in these last days, has a plan for His people. He desires His saints to be in the forefront of what will take place. Even now God is raising up men and women who have a heart after Him. These trail blazers will be sold out to God and begin to stand up for what is right.

The Lord has been impressing upon me that He is raising up a **Shadrach, Meshach, and Abednego Generation**. This will be an army of people who would rather die than compromise. Shadrach, Meshach, and Abednego had boldness not many have today. They stood up for what they believed regardless of the consequences, or what others thought of them. God is placing a holy boldness in His people, so they won't concern themselves in 'going with the flow' for the sake of popularity or acceptance. They'll stand up! Like Shadrach, Meshach, and Abednego, they'll declare the faithfulness of God regardless of their situation. Yes, persecution will come to them, but God will see them through as He did the three young Hebrew men.

This army of people will manifest a maturity birthed through the hard times they face. Their testimonies will touch the hearts of numerous people. They'll be thankful for the mighty hand of God's faithfulness. And the world will be shocked at what these trail blazers will do for God!

What a challenge to follow the example of Shadrach, Meshach, and Abednego. I believe their uncompromising holy boldness is available to everyone who asks. God's grace will see you through – even through flames of fire if need be – **if** you're willing to pay the price of not bowing down to the ways of this world.

28

# OVERCOMING YOUR PAST

One of the biggest drawbacks to sharing faith today is that many feel they must totally fix themselves up <u>before</u> they can tell others the Good News. Don't surmise that one day you'll be a perfect saint <u>then</u> you can go out and share Christ. You'll never be absolutely perfect. This doesn't mean as I said before you can deliberately live in sin and rebellion and expect God to use you. You must be different from the world and demonstrate <u>by your life</u>, that you have "something better" to offer them. If you have made a commitment to God, and given your life to Him, you can be used of God. Sure you'll make mistakes in your Christian walk, **"For our righteousness is as filthy rags" (Isaiah 64:6)**, but we must move on, asking forgiveness for our sin, striving always to be better, and continue to reach out to others.

In this chapter I'm dealing with <u>"overcoming the effects of the past."</u>

I believe this subject is so important that I dedicate a majority of the section to this subject.

Many people struggle with reaching out in boldness, because of their former life. Satan has them so bound up in their past, they feel they can't be <u>effective</u> in changing their world for Jesus. They mistakenly perceive themselves as unworthy and useless. Living in "a yesterday world", they hold on to their sin rather than giving it to God once and for all. I believe God desires to set you free from the chains of your past so you may make a difference in your world.

**In Philippians chapter 3, verse 10-14 it reads, "<u>That I might know him, and the power of his resurrection</u>, and the fellowship of his sufferings. Being made conformable unto his death; If by any means I might obtain unto the resurrection of the dead. Not as though I had already attained, either were al-**

**ready perfect: but I follow after, If that I may apprehend that for which I am apprehended of Christ Jesus. Brethren, I count not myself to have apprehended: but this one thing I do, <u>Forgetting those things which are behind, and reaching forth unto those things which are before. I press toward the mark for the prize of the high calling of God in Christ Jesus.</u>"**

Paul had every reason not to become involved in changing his world. He was a killer of Christians, a murderer influenced by false religious doctrine. Paul referred to himself as "chief of all sinners." **(1 Timothy 1:15 b).** From man's perspective he had no right to ever call himself a Christian. God was faithful, though, in Paul's life to forgive him, and use him mightily in ministry. This murderer-turned-apostle, wrote over half of the New Testament. In order for Paul to be useful to God, he had to put the tormenting images of his past behind him and move forward. I'm sure Satan seized every opportunity to remind him of his past sin. <u>Paul had to choose not to entertain those thoughts, but move on.</u> Paul didn't let his past stop him! Neither should you!

Many people cannot positively affect their world, due to the pull of their past, because they believe the many lies of Satan. You must realize God wants to place His power and anointing within you, and powerfully use you to Invade the darkness *regardless of your past.* Many of you reading this now are only functioning below par, because you refuse to let go of your past. You haven't received God's complete forgiveness. You don't believe Jesus <u>will</u> forgive you. You may say *"I believe that if I confess my sins He will forgive me,"* but actually down deep in your heart, you haven't truly believed God <u>has</u> forgiven you. You may also consider your sin (s) too big for the Father to erase. You may even have repented of that same sin five minutes ago. How does God forgive us? It is only by His <u>grace</u> and <u>mercy.</u> God's grace – His unmerited favor – is so hard to understand at times, but thankfully – His grace is always there for us. **(2 Cor. 1 :3)**

In my own life I struggled mightily with my past. I used to tell the Lord all the time, *How could I mess up like that?* It would really bother me, because I often fell in the same trap. I did the things I didn't want to do and didn't do the things I should have done. Yes, I wanted to be free from my mistakes, but I didn't know how to receive God's total forgiveness. The Lord had to remind me He has forgiven me, and remembers my sins no more. Does that mean I should do whatever I want because God's going to forgive me? No way! We never use God's grace and mercy for a license for our own rebellion. But, it's comforting to know when we do mess up God is faithful to forgive our sins and cleanse us from all unrighteousness. **(1 Jn 1:9)**

One of the biggest weapons Satan uses against us is **the past. (Isaiah 54:17)** He reminds anointed people especially, of all their sin. He attacks their minds with discouragement. **(Eph. 6)** Satan's a big bully and loves to make you feel like a "no-good heathen." Always remember, it was **Jesus** who took the stripes upon His back. It was **Jesus** who took the thorn's upon His head, and the bruises on His body. It was **Jesus** who was crucified that I may have forgiveness of all sin. **(Isaiah 53:5)** It's not what you do to receive forgiveness of sin, but what has already been done long ago. God is a holy God, He cannot look at sin. He decreed all sin must be paid for by death. **(Rom. 6:23)** Jesus volunteered to pay that ultimate price – by giving His life for us. You might say **Jesus took our bullet**. Jesus said on the cross, "it is finished." He didn't say "oh there's much more to come." "It is finished" means that all my sins have been paid for. Hallelujah! The cross made it final – all sin could be forgiven regardless of how evil it is.

Because of the cross, God will forgive you as much as He is willing to forgive me, or anyone else. God doesn't have some big scale up in heaven weighing how big your sin is in order to see if He will forgive you. No, God forgives all sin the same. All sin is like indelible ink. The stain won't come out by any natural means. **The only way the stain of sin can be removed is by the blood of Je-**

**sus**. His blood can remove any sin no matter how big and dark the stain. Realizing this promise and not excepting God's forgiveness for your sins, is like stepping on the cross of Christ. What your actually saying is *"Jesus what you did on the cross is not good enough for me because my sin is special and I'm an exception."* If this is your attitude precious one, God desires to set you free. Will you let Him?

Did you know you can actually stifle the power and holy boldness God has placed within you – by not excepting God's forgiveness? It will not flow through you as it should, because your eyes are upon yourself and not fixed on God. The power of God only flows when you are **God-ward** not **self-ward.** Another trap Satan employs is to try to turn you aside from the right path by getting your eyes off the road. He accomplishes this by throwing your past in your face, hoping you'll wallow in your problems rather than be used of God. Precious one, do not be ignorant of Satan's tactics. **(2 Cor. 2:11)** Self-centeredness is like a dam holding you back. Allow the blood of Jesus to destroy that dam. Let God's power flow through you to the fullest potential. Satan's main goal is to destroy your faith and your love toward God, by telling you lies. **(Jn 10:10)** Choose this very day not to believe them. Instead, believe what God has to say. What God has to say is truth, and that truth will set you free!

Satan may strive to convince you that God is a **"big cosmic mean-ie"** up in heaven who is angry with you. If you accept his lie, he's won the battle. The power of God, that holy boldness will not be yours. God doesn't carry around a big club just waiting to bring up your past and knock you over the head with it. Remember it is Satan who comes to steal and kill and destroy. **(Jn. 10:10). Jesus** comes to bring <u>life</u> and that more abundantly. Satan's agenda – throwing your past in your face and warping your view of God's love – will stifle the power of God in your life. But, listen up, there's good news. You <u>can</u> be set free from your past and I want to tell you how.

The Lord laid upon my heart **five keys that will help you get free from the past..** If you struggle with your past; if accepting God's forgiveness is a problem for you – then take these five keys and begin to use them and put them into practice in your life. Stand back and see what God will do.

**Key number one – <u>Ask God for a revelation of the Blood.</u>**

If you have a true revelation, which means you have <u>an unveiling of the truth, or you see something in a fresh new way,</u> you'll be set free from the past. If you could truly understand what Jesus went through for you on the cross, I believe you would unreservedly accept God's forgiveness for your past deeds. Just think about this for a moment.

**Jesus left a glorious heaven**

**Jesus was confined to an earthly body**

**Jesus related to mankind completely**

**Jesus volunteered to pay the price for their sin**

**(Phil. 2:7,8)**

He lived on this earth for 33 years and died a terrible death for us. I would like to describe for you all that Jesus went through for you at Calvary that you may never again wonder if Jesus truly loves you and is willing to forgive all sin.

God's all consuming love for us was decisively demonstrated at the cross. **Isaiah fifty-three, verse ten, says it pleased the Lord to bruise Jesus and give Him grief.** God let His love for mankind overcome and surpass His feelings of grief for His son. Even knowing the brutal and most excruciating manner in which Jesus would carry the sins of the world, God still allowed His son to be the atoning sacrifice for the world – **for us!**

I don't think most Christians realize what Jesus went through for them. People often picture this "wimpy" looking Jesus on a cross with a few scratches on Him. What a misconception. Jesus had a human body just like you and me. He felt pain just as we do. When Jesus was hung upon the cross, He didn't even look like a man. He was so bruised and bloody His features could not be recognized.

Crucifixion was the Roman death penalty for non-citizen slaves, foreigners, and criminals. It was the most agonizing and dishonorable death a brutal and barbarous empire could devise. Nails were driven in through the hands and feet to a wooden cross. The victim was left hanging for days in complete agony, suffering both starvation and unquenchable thirst.

Crucifixion was not the only painful thing the Lord had to endure for us. He was whipped beforehand with a whip called the "**Cat of Nine tails.**" It was the Roman tool of torture. Made up of nine strands of strong, thick leather cord, laced with pieces of metal, rock, wood and other sharp objects, it would literally rip the victim to shreds. Each time the whip reached its victim, it would literally rap around the body. At that time the captors would pull it. This action would cause a breaking of arteries and veins, plus a ripping away of anything in its path, such as eyes. Many times the prisoner would not survive the flogging. **Jesus was whipped by soldiers over 30 times.** All through this savage flogging, He never once cursed at the soldiers. After His whipping, all that was left of Jesus was one massive piece of loose flesh.

That's not all! Upon His head was slammed a crown of thorns. The length of each individual thorn was two to four inches – long enough to cause plenty of damage. Jesus must have had unimaginable pain as that crown was brutally shoved on His head by the soldiers.

As if that wasn't enough, Jesus was forced to drag a big heavy cross to the **Place of the Skull** (Mt. 27:33), also known as **Calva-**

**ry or Golotha. (Mt. 27:33).** It took a real man to go through what Jesus did. Not some skinny little Jesus, but a big strong man with a heart full of love for us.

Jesus was mocked, scoffed at, jeered and railed on by the chief priests, elders, scribes, and soldiers. He faced a hard-hearted, contemptible crowd that wanted Him dead more than anything else. The Roman garrison with about five to six hundred men all joined in on the mockery and torment of Jesus. They hit Him. They spit upon Him. They even yanked out his beard.

He was very much abused while He carried the cross. He carried the cross, and wore the crown down a long hard road. The road that was lined with merciless people that spit and mocked Him. There was only a small crowd that wept for Jesus. But, He silenced them saying, "Weep not for me, But for your children." (Luke 23:28) In Matthew 27:25, the crowd cried out, "His blood be on us and our children." To this day the blood of Jesus is still on the children of the Jews as a result of them yelling this curse upon themselves.

When Jesus reached the place of His crucifixion, they offered Jesus wine mixed with Gall, to stupefy Him before the long nails were driven into His hands and feet. Jesus refused the Gall. The nails that were driven into Him sent convulsions of excruciating pain into His nervous system.

The throbbing pain that Jesus felt was unbearable, and the long hours of torture that followed were incredible. The thirst, starvation, breathing disorders, loss of blood, and the body slowing shutting itself off was an immense trial to go through. Each time He would take a breath He would have to push with His legs, and pull His body upward causing great pain throughout His body. Many times a prisoner would not have the energy to pull himself up to breathe and die from suffocation. For this reason, the legs of the victim were broken to hasten death from lack of air. Death usually followed in four to six days. In Jesus case, it spanned six hours.

Jesus was already dead when the spear pierced His side. Some medical authorities have said that when heart rupture occurs, that blood collects in the pericardium (the heart's wall lining), and often will divide into a watery curium. If this is true, then the reason for Jesus death was heart rupture. Under extreme pain, and the pressure of His wild racing blood, His heart burst. Jesus may have died heartbroken over the sins of mankind and the withdrawal of His Fathers from Him. Darkness fell from noon to three that could symbolize God's back turned on Jesus.

We plainly see the extent God went through for mankind. Allowing His only son to die such a way that He may be raised from the dead for man to be saved. Jesus had to drink the cup of death and in our place. His blood was shed instead of ours.

Now let me ask you a question. Would a God who sent His son to die in the most excruciating manner for the lost world suddenly stop caring for His children? Would He refuse to forgive the very people who his only begotten son agonized and died for? Of course not! God's love for mankind is seen through the cross. God is a loving heavenly Father who desires to wipe away all your past. God, out of the very essence of His nature, never abandons us or flaunts our sin in our face, But is there to forgive who ever will ask. His mercy is new every morning! (Lam 3:22,23) Ask today precious one for a revelation of Jesus blood and cross, and forget your past Jesus has already paid the price for your sin for you. To dwell on your past is to insult God. God is willing and able to forgive, except today that forgiveness from God.

## Key Number Two-<u>Forgive yourself from your past.</u>

One of the hardest things to do is to forgive yourself for your past. Sometimes you have no problem of excepting God's forgiveness, but forgiving yourself is another story. You may feel as if you can not live with yourself because of your past. Many people today are still beating themselves over the head for sins they committed years ago. They can not understand how in the world they could commit such a sin. They may even have made the same mistake time after time and refuse to believe they can change so they do not forgive themselves. The bottom line is <u>God wants you to forgive yourself</u>. If you truly want to be used of God with power and boldness you must forgive yourself. If you want the effects of the past not to effect you please precious one forgive yourself.

When you rehearse and torment your mind with past sins, you are opening the door to Satan. It's as if telling the Devil I enjoy having you around! Not forgiving yourself gives Satan a foothold in your life. God's blessing can not be upon you when you refuse to forgive yourself. Kick the Devil out! Place the blood of Jesus over your mind. The Devil is faithful in only one thing and that is to remind you of your past. Refuse to entertain any thoughts when he reminds you. Tell the Devil to take a hike it's all under the blood! Remind the Devil of his future. Remember when you stand before Jesus there is nothing to fear because you are forgiven. **(1 Jn 4:18)** All the sin is removed and when God sees you he sees Jesus because of the blood. The blood covers your imperfections. It is as God put on blood sun shades and only sees Jesus. Do not fear but forgive yourself and remind the Devil of this truth. This truth alone will send him running in terror! **(James 4:7)**

**Key Number Three**- Forget your past. It is impossible to be bold for God when you play your past in theater of your mind over and over again. The more you play it the more you will feel condemned. In **Romans 8:1 it reads "Therefore, there is now no condemnation for those who are in Christ Jesus, because through Christ Jesus the law of the Spirit of life set me free from the law of sin and death."** The spirit never brings condemnation on a believer, but brings conviction to the heart. **Hebrews 12:5-11 reads "My son, do not make light of the Lord's discipline, and do not lose heart when he rebukes you, 6) <u>because the Lord disciplines those he loves</u>, and punishes everyone he accepts as a son. 7) Endure hardship as discipline; God is treating you as sons. For**

what son is not disciplined by his father? 8) If you are not disciplined (and everyone undergoes discipline), then you are il-
legitimate children and not true sons. 9) Moreover, we have all
had human fathers who disciplined us and we respected them
for it. How much more should we submit to the Father of our
spirits and live! 10) Our fathers disciplined us for a little while
as they thought best; but God disciplines us for our good, that
we may share in his holiness. 11) No discipline seems pleas-
ant at the time, but painful. Later on, however, <u>it produces a
harvest</u> of righteousness and peace for those who have been
trained by it.

The work of the Holy Spirit is to correct, but he never does it to
destroy. Condemnation always brings down a person not build
them up. **John 10:10 "The thief (Satan) comes to kill steal and
destroy; I come that they may have life, and have it to the full."**
Satan's three fold plan for your life is Steal from you to kill you
and to ultimately destroy you. One way he does this through condemnation. The Holy Spirit always <u>convicts</u> this brings life and
not death! Yes, God's correction can hurt at times, but it is always
done to better the person out of love, not leave a person feeling
worthless and hopeless.

**Condemnation = Judgment not based on love, but is meant to
push down**

**Conviction = Correction from God that builds up**

Replaying your past over and over again in theater of your mind
will only let condemnation creep in your life. Forgetting your past
can only be done by accepting God's forgiveness and moving on.
You cannot drive down the road looking through your rear view
mirror and you cant go through life being consumed by your past.
It reads in **Micah 7:19 "He will turn again, he will have compassion upon us; he will subdue our sins."** What does the word
subdue mean? <u>To subdue something means we beat it down, we</u>

get rid of it, we deminish it or smash it. What the bible is saying is God takes all our sins and smashes them up and destroys them and throws them into the sea. Cory Ten Boom put it this way. **"God takes all our sins and throws them into the deepest ocean and puts a big sign that says 'No Fishing.'"**. Don't be like so many Christians that ask forgiveness, but refuses to forget they keep going back to that sea with their fishing rod and take back everything that just gave to God.

Satan also loves to come along and get you all depressed into the depths of despair. So many times when I get down I give myself a pity party and sing that song my mom used to joke **"Nobody likes me everybody hates me I guess I will go eat worms."**: The problem is we really do not eat those worms we go fishing with them into the sea of forgetfulness. Stop fishing in you past and playing those past movies in your mind and start renewing your mind with the Word of God and His promises. Stop putting junk into your mind about all your past defeats this will only stifle the power of God flowing through us. The Bible reads in **Romans 12:2 "Do not conform any longer to the pattern of this world, but be transformed by the renewing of your mind. then you will be able to test and approve what God's will is-his good, pleasing and perfect will."** Transforming the mind by reading the Word and carefully placing in positive things that are good. **Phillippians 4:8 "Finally, brothers, whatever is true, whatever is noble, whatever is right, whatever is pure, whatever is lovely, whatever is admirable-if anything is excellent or praiseworthy-think about such things."** There are great teaching tapes and wonderful anointed preaching videos that will minister to you and help renew your mind. Also we have countless Christian books available to read. Personally, I think that the more you read the word and other Christian books the stronger your spirit becomes. Let me encourage you teenager to wash your mind with the word you cannot go wrong!

**Number Four: Forgive others who hurt you**

Many times getting free from our past can be difficult because other people have caused severe pain. Has someone hurt you deeply? As long as you refuse to forgive, you drag that person through life with you. You can only be released from that person when you forgive them. The word "forgive" means to give something. You are giving that person freedom from being indebted to you. You then receive peace in your heart.

In Ephesians 4:32

**"Instead, be kind and merciful, and forgive anyone who does wrong, just as Christ has forgiven you. Love is more important than anything else. It is what ties everything completely together."**

If we expect God to forgive us of all our sins, (and we all sin and fall short everday of His glory (Romans 3:23) then we too must forgive and forget. Refusing to forgive only hurts ourselves. You are the one who loses in the end. Unforgiveness always turns to bitterness. Bitterness destroys a person if not dealt with.

**Number 5 Embrace God's forgiveness and let Him set you free**

Only through Jesus can the effects of the past be changed. He desires to set every person free from their past. You can begin by:

( Ask God for a fresh discovery of the blood.

( Forgive Yourself.

( Forget the past.

( Forgive others that have hurt you.

( Embrace God's forgiveness and letting Him set you free.

**Personal Reflection:**

Have you made a fresh discovery of the blood?

Have you forgiven yourself from your past mistakes?

Do you continue to criticize yourself for your past?

Do you play reruns of your mistakes in your mind?

Have you released others who have hurt you?

Do you embrace God's forgiveness every day and know you are special to Him?

How do you perceive God to be after you ask forgiveness?

# SECTION 2
# Evangelism Hall of Fame

# SICKLE OF HARVEST

**"Thrust in your sickle and reap, for the time has come for You to reap for the harvest of the earth is ripe."** Revelation 14; 15

This scripture speaks of the **'Son of Man'** being the Reaper.

An instrument of harvest – the sickle is "a reaping hook." In a very real sense **the evangelist** who goes forth in the calling of the Master – is also reaping the "precious fruit of the earth."

In the hands of the evangelist (the sent one) – the reaping hook is **The Word of God** – preached forcefully with such authority and might – in the **power of the Spirit** – that indeed a harvest of souls are gathered for the Kingdom.

Ever since the fall of man, even after God's great flood of judgment, people on Planet Earth have progressively degenerated and traveled far afield from the Father's dream of us being a family.

Humankind, is still hopelessly entangled with the cunning and deceitful "destroyer." We persistently engage in ongoing rebellion – following after other gods – gods disguised in the trappings of wealth and status, human reasoning and self-indulgence. Despite the enormity of this mass defiance of His created ones – **God devised an effective Plan B.**

Over and over the compassionate, long-suffering Creator has called us back, pleading with us – *"not willing that any should perish."* **Jesus came! Jesus restored! Jesus conquered! Jesus commissioned!**

The prime agents of God's steady pursuit of His human creation have been **the evangelists.** Various meanings of the word "evangelist" have included apostle, clergyman, messenger etc.

**Evangelism** is said to be one of the highest of divine callings. This "reaching out" – was authorized by our Lord Jesus Christ. It was He who commissioned his disciples to: ***"Go into all the world and preach the gospel to every creature – beginning in Jerusalem." "...repentance and remission of sins should be preached in His name to all nations, beginning at Jerusalem."*** Mark 16:15 – Luke 24:47

**And go they did!** Over the centuries, treading the landscapes of the world's lost – a consecrated army of selfless men and women – have courageously battled for the kingdom of God.

These faithful pioneers passed the Gospel torch lit by the Master Himself – to generations following.

Abbreviated chronicles of some of the more renowned **heroes of THE FAITH,** past and present – are here introduced.

### THE HEROES:

# BILLY GRAHAM

### A Legend in His Own Time

How do you measure greatness?

Of many prevalent definitions this familiar adage is particularly apropos:

"Only one life twill soon be past; only what's done for Christ will last." Those brief, but profound words may well characterize the ongoing legacy of **world-renown evangelist Billy Graham.**

A dynamo crusader for the cause of **Jesus Christ**, Billy's all-consuming passion in life has been to bring the lost to the Savior – "just as they are." Countless millions in more than 185 nations can trace their soul's salvation to his compelling preaching.

The story of this towering ambassador for God began humbly in the southern locale of Charlotte, North Carolina. **William Franklin Graham Junior's first lusty cry made the airwaves on November 7, 1918.** He was born on the rural dairy farm of his Scotch parents William Franklin Graham and Morrow Coffee Graham.

The Grahams were devout adherents of the Presbyterian faith. Their family altar was a tradition kept alive from the earliest days of their marriage. Bible study was a daily regimen. In view of the future events, it is conceivable that his mother – like the biblical Hannah did with Samuel – offered her infant son to the service of the Lord.

It was a chaotic time, what with the ravages of World War I to repair and the recent communist uprising of Bolshevik Russia. Moreover, Billy grew up in the segregated South and came to young manhood in the shadows of the Depression.

Prohibition was repealed in 1933. Prior to its demise, Billy's father had been a strong prohibition supporter. Warding off any future involvement with alcohol, he literally forced Billy and his sister to consume beer until they were becoming ill. With that he urged his children – when confronting their friends offering them alcohol – to reply thus: "just tell them you've already tasted it and you don't like it. That's all the reason you need to give." Not surprising, Billy has remains a teetotaler to this day.

Wavy-haired, tall and lanky, Billy at fifteen was still uncertain of his place in a runaway world. He couldn't possibly imagine that one day he'd be given an enviable niche in God's Hall of Fame. But the Lord would soon open doors that would dramatically change the course of his life.

An on-fire preacher named Dr. Mordecai Fowler Ham (who had a reputation for renewing religious fervor and for wooing young people from adolescent rebellion) was invited to Charlotte to hold revival meetings. Billy appeared uninterested.

Dr. Ham had alleged there was "house of immorality" located near Charlotte's Central High School, was being frequented daily at lunch time by some of the students. His accusations, played up in the Charlotte News, drew student threats of a protest march and personal bodily harm.

One of his friends invited Billy to "come out and hear our fighting preacher." The word fighter got his attention. "I like a fighter" said Billy. He went to a meeting and on that night was filled with awe at the power behind Dr. Ham's message. Writing much later in his autobiography, Billy observed, "I was hearing another voice, as was often said of Dwight L. Moody when he preached: the voice of the Holy Spirit."

Billy subsequently attended many of Dr. Ham's meetings. In the interim Billy turned sixteen. One unforgettable night shortly after his birthday, Dr. Ham, closing his message, gave his customary invitation. He quoted the scripture in Romans 5:8, *"But God commends his love toward us, in that, while we were yet sinners, Christ died for us."*

Two songs were sung as they waited for people to respond. As the last verse was being sung, Billy, accompanied by hundreds of others, went forward and stood at the front of the stage.

For some people the moment they surrender their lives to Christ is highly charged and emotional. For Billy Graham it was not. In his own words, recorded by biographer William Martin in "A Prophet with Honor," he said:

"I didn't have any tears, I didn't have any emotion, I didn't hear any thunder, there was no lightning...But right there, I made my decision for Christ. It was simple as that, and as conclusive." Billy's friend Grady Wilson and his brother T.W. were also converted that night and all three young men are ministers today.

The now committed Billy Graham would later be educated in three colleges – Bob Jones College, the Florida Bible Institute and the highly respected Wheaton College in Chicago.

**God has a way of divinely orchestrating the lives of those He has called to His service.** For Billy this would be amply proven. Paul Fischer, a Chicago lawyer had been so impressed with Billy's preaching, that during his last year at Florida Bible Institute, he offered to pay his first year tuition at Chicago's prestigious Wheaton College. A grateful Billy did apply to Wheaton and was accepted.

When Billy was about to graduate from Florida Bible Institute in May 1940, the traditional Class Night prophecy was given just before Commencement. Original in its content and duly prayed over by class members, that prophecy was read as follows:

*Each time God had a chosen human instrument to shine forth His light in the darkness. Men like Luther, John and Charles Wesley,*

*Moody and others were ordinary men, but men who heard the voice of God. Their surrounding conditions were as black as night, but they had God. "If God is for us, who can be against us?" (Romans 8:31). It has been said that Luther revolutionized the world. It was not he, but Christ working through him. The time is ripe for another Luther, Wesley, Moody — — — — —. There is a challenge facing us.*

**Those words were amazingly prophetic indeed. Although no one knew it then, a North Carolina country boy named Billy Graham would one day be added to that list of honor.**

On December 7th, 1941 the day President Roosevelt said would "live in infamy" – the Japanese attacked the American naval station at Pearl Harbor in Hawaii. With that attack the bloody and long lasting World War II was launched. America would be at the forefront of battle.

Being a minister, Billy wanted to serve in the military as a chaplain. It was imperative however, for him to finish his degree first, so he remained at Wheaton. That decision would deeply affect his life. For it was there that he met the attractive hazel-eyed Ruth Bell. Born in China, Ruth was the daughter of Christian missionaries and grew up in Asia. She herself aspired to become a missionary to Tibet.

Billy and Ruth began dating and a mere few months later Billy proposed. These two earnest young Christians both graduated with a degree in theology in 1943. They were married that summer on Friday, August 13th. Firmly grounded on **the rock Christ Jesus –** their marriage was to last for 63 years and produce 5 children.

Not long after their marriage, Billy assumed his first and only pastorate – the Village Church of Western Springs, Illinois. During his brief tenure there he helped double weekly church attendance to more than a hundred.

The war then being in its closing days, Billy's long held hope for the chaplaincy faded. Divine providence however, would take him down another path all together, affording him exciting new opportunities.

The young Billy Graham had thus far achieved a small measure of success guiding the flock of Village Church. The hand of God would soon extend his sphere of influence yet again.

**Billy was offered a radio show** pre-planned by a local radio minister, who because of time constraints was unable to record. He accepted. It proved a strategic asset in his overall ministry. Later on, 210 of his radio messages on "The Hour of Decision" were in print and available to the general public.

Initially sponsored by the church, Billy's program became hugely popular. As a result he was called to other areas and held numerous evangelistic outreaches. Unfortunately, the burgeoning demands upon his time and service, conflicted with his multifaceted duties as a pastor. Ultimately Billy stepped down. **He would opt to serve the Lord as a full-time career evangelist.**

Another opportunity for furthering the Gospel was granted Billy when he was asked to organize the fledgling ministry of **Youth for Christ International.** Again he accepted. Billy's energy appeared boundless. As did his seemingly unorthodox methods of presenting the "glad tidings."

Subsequent Youth for Christ rallies, dubbed by some as "Christian vaudeville" were somewhat criticized for their implementation of quiz shows, animal and band performances – anything to command the engagement of the young people.

The censure did little to diminish this vigorous outreach to the youth of the nation and beyond. These meetings were immensely popular.

An estimated million youth attended these rallies across the country every week and their impact was inestimable. From the lips of Billy Graham would issue the words of the Master – filtered through his early training that echoed the integrity, responsibility and hard work ethic of his godly parents.

Meanwhile, Billy's own spirituality was growing deeper and higher. **"I want the fullness of the Holy Spirit."** So said a seeking Billy Graham to Stephen Olford, a minister he'd just heard speak.

Heretofore, Billy had been traveling in Europe with the Youth for Christ team since spring of 1946 – doing the work of an evangelist with his customary fervor. Now it was October. During a soul-challenging meeting at Hildenborough Hall in Kent, Stephen Olford had captured Billy's undivided attention, with his sermon text – *"Be not drunk with wine, wherein is excess; but be filled with the Spirit."* Ephesians 5:18.

Realizing he was lacking the experience the preacher had described, Billy approached Olford after the service. Being very honest, he told the minister he would have been first to respond, had Olford extended an invitation. **"You've spoken of something I don't have. I want the fullness of the Holy Spirit in my life too."**

Since Billy was scheduled to preach in Wales, the two men met nearby a short time later and poured over the Scriptures all day. During his strict upbringing, his parents saw to it that their children memorized hundreds of scriptures that were thoroughly mined for meaning and discussed every day. As a result, Billy had a deep reverence for the Bible and firmly believed in its absolute authority. That divine authority would, without digression, characterize his life and ministry.

Now thoroughly convinced of his own need for the power of the Spirit, Billy asked the Lord for "the anointing You've given my brother." Stephen Olford spent the next day with Billy also. The minister instructed Billy in-depth on how to be filled with the Spir-

51

it and how vital it was to be continually submitted to the Spirit's indwelling. Billy was openly receptive. The Lord's promise of this "power from on high" came alive in his heart that day.

**When these two men knelt in prayer the very presence of God was manifested in that room. An ecstatic Billy exclaimed, "I have it I'm filled." My heart is so flooded with the Holy Spirit." In those momentous hours Billy Graham reached a significant milestone in his walk with the Lord. His experience generated a power soon to be the hallmark of his ministry.**

Preaching that same night at a large Welsh Baptist church, Billy's new anointing bore immediate fruit. Jamming the aisles to reach the front, most of the congregation came forward. As Olford predicted when later relating those events to his father – **the world would soon hear from one fireball preacher – William Franklin Graham.**

Some 30 years later, Dr. Graham would write **"The Holy Spirit"**– a definitive life-changing volume subtitled "Activating God's Power in Your Life." His book would cover a variety of applications diligently authenticated by the Bible. It included the breadth of his own early questions and detailed his personal spiritual experience.

Admittedly, no one can put the Holy Spirit in a literary box, anymore than the ocean can be contained in a wooden barrel. However, for the serious seeker his treatise would "help the reader to discover and implement God's power." Clarifying his purpose in writing it, Dr. Graham said, **"I'm convinced that to be filled with the Holy Spirit is not an option, but a necessity. The Spirit-filled life is not abnormal; it is the normal Christian life."**

He returned to the United States in 1947. Billy's "campaign" (as he called it) focused on the cities of Grand Rapids, Michigan and Charlotte, North Carolina.

During that same year, after a speaking engagement in Minneapolis, Minnesota at Northwestern Schools – the school president Dr. W. B. Riley prophesied that Billy (then only in his late twenties), was earmarked to become the next school president. This would be an honor indeed for one so young and having only an undergraduate degree.

**What a challenge!** When the eminent Dr. Riley passed away at 86 on December 5th 1947 – the board of directors recognized his request by nominating Billy for the presidency of Northwestern Schools. Billy accepted. After five years of directing and vastly improving the school, Billy ended his tenure and moved on.

Before Billy's resignation from the school however, his career would be given an unexpected boost. The year 1949 would prove a banner year for the earnest young crusader in more ways than one. During that time Billy's energies were concentrated on campaigns in four major American cities – Baltimore, Miami, Altoona and Los Angeles. Events in the last city would prove the catalyst for significant and vastly advantageous change.

The organization of "Christ for Greater Los Angeles" had scheduled a 3-week revival in late September. They contacted Billy asking him to speak there. He was also invited to Beverly Hills where he spoke to a number of Hollywood's famous. It was there that Stuart Hamlin, host of a popular radio show, cordially invited Billy to appear on his show, which he did. Stuart then enthusiastically told his audience to attend Billy's tent meetings saying that he was going himself – much to Billy's surprise.

**The Lord has a wonderful way of taking a person's life and creating a masterpiece, event by event, person by person and prayer by prayer. This was amply evident in the life of Billy Graham. Because of Billy's willingness to be led and shaped by the Master Sculptor – miracles large and small – would attend his way.**

True to his word, Stuart Hamlin attended those meetings. Repeatedly however, because of his inner turmoil he would angrily walk out. His heart wrestled with what Billy was preaching and the conviction of the Holy Spirit.

Finally one very early morning, Stuart stopped resisting. An awakened Billy met him in the lobby at his request. Previously alerted by Billy – his wife Ruth and their friends, the Wilsons covered the two men with prayer. Billy and Stuart talked and prayed together as he introduced him to the Lord Jesus. **Responding to the altar call at the next evening's service was one changed Stuart Hamlin.**

**Stuart later wrote the ever-popular hymn:**

**"It is no secret what God can do. What he's done for others He'll do for you….."** Because God was so obviously working in that campaign it was extended.

Public interest was growing, especially after Stuart Hamlin gave his testimony on radio. One night an abundance of reporters and photographers flocked to the tent. "Why are you here all of a sudden?" Billy's question was answered in a surprising way.

It seems the influential newspaper baron **William Randolph Hearst** had been informed of Billy's appeal for national restoration of spiritual values.

How had he heard? Had the newspaper mogul secretly checked out Billy Graham's hard-line soul-winning agenda? Or had he sent an underling as some supposed? Perhaps with age and his checkered career spiraling down, he looking to assuage his own spiritual battleground. Hard telling.

Whatever the reason, Hearst believed Graham's message to be timely and necessary, and decided to help him get it out. With Hearst's two words of command to his media empire – "Puff Graham" – headline stories highlighting the Graham campaign appeared in the Hearst-owned Los Angeles Examiner and Los Angeles Herald Express and elsewhere. Other major city newspapers picked up the story and Billy's new, larger tent was packed.

**The Los Angeles crusade lasted eight weeks. By its end, untold thousands had attended to hear Graham and receive Jesus. Lives were dramatically changed. And Billy Graham had been catapulted from mediocrity to the limelight of national prominence.**

Leaning heavily on the Lord's guidance, Billy had been satisfied with wherever God had sent him. To him souls were the principle thing – garnering souls for the kingdom was all that mattered.

**But Billy soon realized that God had a bigger vision for him than he previously had for himself. With the fire of the living God in his heart, Billy's passion for souls would one day take him around the world.**

**They had always prayed together, Billy and his wife Ruth.** Prayer was the cement that bonded the fabric of their lives. And Ruth had long ago released him to evangelize wherever God would lead him. Ruth was a remarkably selfless woman. She understood that her husband was compelled to follow the call of God upon his life and that call superceded everything else – even family.

Fully supportive of her husband's mission, Ruth traveled with him whenever possible. Her deep love, faith and steadfastness would be a constant he could depend on. And always, despite her endless personal and family adjustments – she prayed a divine covering over him and the ministry.

During the turbulent times of the King years and the Civil Rights Movement, a belligerent mass of southern (and sometimes northern) bigots perpetually fought the inclusion of 'people of color' on what they regarded as "their turf." The nation was often a cultural war zone.

And where was Billy Graham in all this? The outspoken evangelist was on the frontlines contending with intolerance, discrimination and injustice. Graham steadfastly refused to allow his meetings to be segregated. His strong stand against inequality inevitably cost him some supporters. He took that loss in stride.

**Despite a climate of strife and seething racial unrest, Billy continued to preach the love of God – the God who was "no respecter of persons" – the God who sovereignly invited "whosoever will" to come.**

God had long ago removed any lingering trace of prejudice from Billy's heart. His meetings and his choirs were fully integrated. A veteran stage and screen actress, the golden-voiced, brown-skinned **Ethel Waters** was his featured soloist for decades.

Ethel's dedication to Jesus was legendary, as was her passionate singing – performed at the crusades. Her premier song **"His Eye is on the Sparrow"** moved many an audience to tears. Ethel Waters remained a cherished friend of the Grahams until her death.

**Courageously challenging the mores of the segregated society of his times – Billy Graham assisted the civil rights agenda of his good friend Dr. Martin Luther King.**

Moreover, in 1978 Roman Catholic Poland would hear the rousing salvation messages of Billy Graham in Warsaw, Pozman, Wroclaw, Katowice, Czestochowa and Cracow – with sometimes unexpected results. And the crowds continued to gather. For many of them it was standing room only.

Christ the King Cathedral in Katowice was reputedly the largest church in Poland. Graham preached there to an overflow crowd of 6,500. At the conclusion of each message, thousands accepted Christ.

Initially invited to Poland by the Polish Baptist Union and the Polish Ecumenical Council, Billy Graham was instrumental in forging a new spirit of cooperation. Poland's churches are predominantly Roman -Catholic. Yet, his 'born-again message' was warmly welcomed with many souls being saved and Christians heartened.

During his Polish tour, in addition to preaching, Graham also met with religious and political leaders. He likewise visited many of Poland's national shrines and historical sites.

**He was deeply moved at Auschwitz, one of the infamous Nazi death camps where four million prisoners had died. Shaken by this visible monument to man's inhumanity to man – Dr. Billy Graham would afterward plead with world leaders to learn the lessons of Auschwitz and its staggering barbarism. "Learn the lessons – before another (perhaps nuclear or biochemical) holocaust would snuff out the lives of entire populations."**

After his return to the States, Billy resumed his breathtaking round of crusades. He had much earlier devised a formula for successful revivals and tried to adhere to it as much as possible. Requirements were:

Cooperation with a city's ministerial association.

Involvement in the campaign by many church congregations.

Major use of printing, publicity and advertising.

The use of consecrated music to prepare restless souls.

The supplications of countless praying Christians.

A simple Gospel message adorned with Gospel texts applicable to the times.

**The nonprofit Billy Graham Evangelistic Association (BGEA) formed in1950 was dedicated and highly effective.** Originally headquartered in Minneapolis, the Association was later relocated in Charlotte, North Carolina. The widely circulated Decision Magazine was its official publication.

Besides Billy, the team was comprised of Ruth Graham, the Wilsons – Grady and T.W. and George; song leader Cliff Barrows who directed the mass choirs and his wife Billie a pianist and the inimitable George Beverly Shea. They would work and pray and rejoice over the harvest together for many decades. Grady Wilson was a mainstay. Of course there were also the countless 'behind the scenes' souls who labored so faithfully.

In his book "Then Sings My Soul," Bev Shea remembers when he returned from London, he brought back "How Great Thou Art" – a new hymn given him by his friend George Gray. Instantly popular in America, it would soon be sung all over the world.

**Billy Frank (as he was affectionately called in his earlier years) had grown from an unsure, nail-biting, sometimes stuttering Carolina farm boy to Dr. Billy Graham – the dynamic globe-trotting evangelist who trailed a phenomenal record of "decisions for Christ."**

From the day of Billy's conversion, the fervent prayers of his mother Morrow had beseeched heaven daily for her son to "lift up the cross of Christ and go into the ministry." And heaven had answered – big time!

With every successive campaign, this highly favored ambassador for **the Kingdom of Heaven** was making deep inroads into the dominion of darkness – persistently snatching lost souls as "brands from the burning!"

**Ultimately, the indefatigable Billy Graham would be the friend, confident, advisor and counselor of eleven United States presidents beginning with Harry Truman. For decades, he has been the annual speaker at the President's Prayer Breakfast in the**

**Capital.**

**Because of his ongoing ministry at the White House, George Herbert Walker Bush designated Billy Graham as "America's pastor." It was Billy the family friend, who in 1985 had encouraged the 40-year old George W. to seek salvation as he pointed the way to Christ.**

Billy and Ruth enjoyed a marriage lasting sixty-three fruitful years, A prolific writer and poet, Ruth Bell Graham was eighty-seven when she passed away on June 14th, 2007. Her resting-place is in Charlotte, beside the Billy Graham Library.

At this point in time, we are ending the first decade of the twenty-first century. Known over much of the world, **William Franklin Graham** has spent his life in submission to God's Word and will. With his eyes still riveted on the prize (*"the upward call of God in Christ Jesus"* – Philippians 3: 14) – at

ninety-two years old, it is said he still envisions yet another crusade, though he currently suffers from Parkinson's Disease.

His crusades have been conducted on every continent. He has preached in fifty countries and states. Untold millions have heard the timeless salvation message. And there have been over a million decisions for Christ. His telecasts garner countless viewers. "The Hour of Decision" sustained a veritable multitude of radio listeners.

Billy Graham's writing expertise has gone from widely read newspaper columns to some twenty-seven books, a number of them bestsellers including:

**Just As I Am**

World Aflame

Approaching Hoof-beats

The Holy Spirit

Angel's God's Secret Agents

The Challenge

My Answer

The Secret of Happiness

Peace With God

The Jesus Generation

How to be Born Again

Look to the Hills

Hope for the Troubled Heart

**At different times he had been prevailed upon to run for the U. S. Senate and even the Presidency, but predictably declined both.**

In review – was Billy's evangelistic career all giant steps forward? Hardly. By his own admission, he had more than one "crisis of faith." He relied a lot on Ruth during those times of searing spiritual testing. During Billy's duel-like contests with God – guess who always came out on top?

He maintained a posture of constant vigilance – determined that not even a breath of scandal, would touch himself or his ministry. He was God's man. And God was a god of integrity!

Billy lost some friends along the way. That was to be expected. He grieved much over the defection of his closest friend Charles Templeton, whose controversy with God began at Auschwitz where he became aware of the horrendous Nazi massacre.

"Why did God allow it to happen", he would rail. "Why God?" Chuck's unending rage at that irrevocable injustice continued throughout his years at Princeton. His anger took him from faith to agnosticism and eventually to avowed atheism.

For Billy the hurt of Chuck's falling away never left him. At his dying bedside, Billy stood clasping Chuck's hand, speaking and praying into him Christ's message of forgiveness and restoration. And because his friend never gave up on him – Charles Templeton finally exited the ranks of unbelievers and soon went home to be with the Lord.

**Billy Frank Graham – the country boy turned Christianity's superstar, would come to the ninth decade of his life convinced that he had not besmirched his commission or the name of the God who gave it to him.**

He had not ever betrayed his beloved Ruth or sullied the honored name of Graham. Always he had tried to be an exemplary father, despite his long absences. His children for a little while chose a prodigal path – but eventually like a straight arrow – returned to the fold and the Father who always greeted them with open arms.

**Billy's ministry continues on through his son William Franklin Graham III** an ordained minister and chairman of Samaritan's Purse International and his son Will. Franklin also chairs the Billy Graham Evangelistic Association. Daughter Anne Graham Lotz founded AnGel Ministries and is also an author. She and her husband Dan are parents of three adult children.

Billy resides in a retreat house Ruth had built in Montreat, North Carolina not far from the dairy farm where he was born.

An interesting postscript to the Billy Graham story:

A recent television special toured the amazing Billy Graham Library honoring his life and ministry. A modest Billy takes no credit for it all. "Everything I have has come from the Lord. And I want to give it all back," he said. Arrangements are in the making for his wishes through his son Franklin.

Another telecast highlighted the recently celebrated events of the third Global Congress on World Evangelism. Delegates from 198 countries were in attendance in Capetown. Billy Graham had convened the first such conference in 1974 in Lucerne Switzerland. A live clip of Billy exhorting them at that time stressed: **"The Church has to be mobilized to take the whole Gospel to the whole world – this is our calling."**

**As he awaits his own summons to be with the Lord, Billy Frank Graham looks back on a Christian career of honor. He can take comfort in knowing too that the millions he has shown the way to eternal life can see in him a shining example of what God can do with a yielded life. Billy Graham has a testimony well worth emulating!**

# REINHARD BONNKE

### Reaching Multiplied Millions

**Luke 15: 7** records these words of **Jesus** to the tax collectors, sinners, scribes and Pharisees: *"I say unto you there is more joy in heaven over **one sinner** who repents than over ninety-nine just persons who need no repentance."*

**One sinner!**

Can you imagine the rejoicing going on – with the angels perhaps dancing around heaven – as they watch the **multiplied millions** brought to faith in Jesus Christ as Lord – through the Spirit-filled fire power of **Reinhard Bonnke** during his Great Gospel Crusades?

**Given the history of this pastor/missionary/evangelist it is not surprising that he is known as the "Spiritual Father of Africa." God and Reinhard have a long-standing relationship.**

Billed as a 'German charismatic Christian evangelist', Reinhard Bonnke was born on April 19th 1940 in Konigsberg, East Prussia. Following in the footsteps of his pastor-father, Reinhard committed his life to the Lord Jesus at only nine years of age. Later, while just a youth, he distinctly heard God directing him to go to Africa.

Reinhard underwent preliminary studies at The Bible College of Wales in Swansea. His African ministry would be delayed for seven years as he assumed a Christian pastorate in Germany.

From Germany he left for Africa where he would begin his mission work. God had programmed Reinhard Bonnke for a destiny of a yet unseen magnitude – a calling that would one day astound the world with its impact.

**He was in the small mountain kingdom of Lesotho when the Lord burdened his heart with an amazing vision. He saw the entire continent of Africa "washed in the Blood of Jesus" – from the cities of Cape Town to Cairo and from Dakar to Djibouti. Reinhard 'saw in the Spirit' a vast host of precious souls being reached with the saving Gospel of Jesus, validated with signs following.**

He started out in a tent holding 800 people. When attendance mushroomed rapidly, a mobile structure to seat 34,000 people was commissioned. Unbelievably – attendance at Bonnke's meetings would exceed even that. Open-air Gospel Campaigns followed, gathering together 150,000 people at the outset.

Subsequent citywide meetings would draw some 1, 600,000 attending at once. Sound systems, that could be heard for miles, were of great height.

**"Christ For The Nations (CfaN) was founded by Reinhard Bonnke more than 35 years ago.** Besides its office in Africa, this international ministry has offices in the United States, Canada, Australia, Germany, United Kingdom, Hong Kong and Singapore. From the beginning of the 21st century alone – this ministry has recorded decisions for Christ totaling some 50 million!

Other important ministries sponsored by **CfaN** include:

A discipleship training program

CfaN literature = nearly 200 million copies

In 103 languages – have been printed in

54 countries and disseminated around the world.

Additionally, Reinhard Bonnke's 'School of Fire' offers a self-study Holy Spirit Evangelism course for either a certificate or university credits.

Bonnke hosts "Fire Conferences" in various countries – to equip leaders and laborers of the Church for the work of evangelism. He has also distributed to homes worldwide, more than 95,500,000 copies of a salvation message entitled "From Minus to Plus."

His "Full Flame Film Series (several years in the making), challenges the Church to aim for Holy Spirit Evangelism Of the many books authored by Reinhard Bonnke, 178 million copies have been published in 158 languages. A large number of these have been made available at no charge.

Bonnke's evangelical meetings and five-day crusades overall have seen an incredible harvest of conversions to Christ – an estimated 100 + million people!

**How does he do it? How does Bonnke inspire millions upon millions of people to invite Jesus into their lives and choose to walk the path of a Christ one?**

An observer of his ministry would have to say he is – for want of a better simile – like the proverbial horse with blinders. He is focused. When he looks at people, he only sees souls for the Kingdom – whether those souls are in Africa or any other community in the world.

**In his own words Reinhard Bonnke directs would-be evangelists to – "GO!"**

*"Whom shall I send? And who will go for us?"*

says God in Isaiah 6"8.

In the spirit of the prophet Isaiah who told God

"here I am send me"– Bonnke says "realize

that God will send anybody willing."

He further states: "Take the gospel to anyone and it convinces them they have always needed it. Even if they have never heard of Christ, they need him and know it when the gospel reaches them."

**"Preaching is not sermonizing. We don't deliver sermons – we deliver people. The gospel is not reformation, renovation or decoration, but Liberation. Jesus didn't come to make life in prison bearable. He came to set the captives free."**

"Keep preaching the Gospel! Preaching Christ creates the market for salvation, and Jesus saves "completely" – Hebrews 7:25. The Bible is for people who have no faith, to give them faith."

Bonnke believes in essence, that as we "go" as we plunge into the depths of soul-winning – the very power and energy of our Lord Jesus is tapped into us! We develop spiritual muscles as God directs our "on the job training."

**Reinhard Bonnke's dedication to preaching the Gospel with "signs following" – received a divine confirmation with a modern-day Lazarus miracle in December of 2001.**

Nigerian Daniel Ekechukwu and his friend Kingsley Iruka had taken a gift goat to his father who lived outside of the town of Owerri. On the return trip while traveling downhill on a steep road, Daniel's 20-year old Mercedes' brakes failed. The unstoppable vehicle crashed into a stone pillar.

Though shocked, Kingsley was miraculously relatively unhurt. But Daniel had been severely injured with blood pouring from his nose and he was vomiting blood from heavy internal hemorrhage.

Later, at the local Owerri Regional Hospital where he had been taken by ambulance – his wife Nneka listened to his last whispered words before he lapsed into unconsciousness. Medical staff certified Daniel was dead.

Thereafter, Daniel Ekechukwu was embalmed, but without removing his organs as is customary in America. They have no refrigeration so chemicals were injected into his body to slow the decaying process.

Although in shock at Daniel's sudden death, Nneka refused to accept her husband's demise as final. Appearing to some as irrational, she claimed for herself Hebrews 11 – *"Women received their dead raised to life again."*

So convinced was Nneka that God would bring Daniel back to life again, she later persuaded the local mortuary to permit her to move his body to the church in Ontisha, where Reinhard Bonnke was preaching the service that Sunday.

Three days after his accident, Ekechukwu's body was taken from its coffin and laid on a table in the conference center at the Ontisha church. Several pastors gathered together and prayed. They were astonished to see as they prayed, this man start to breathe again. Since this occurred in the church basement while Bonnke was preaching upstairs, he was unaware of what had happened.

Ekechukwu's remarkable resurrection and testimony is well documented in Bonnke's Christ For All Nations (CfaN) 45-minute video released by the ministry.

**The church's senior pastor (Pat Nwachkuw Sr.), told the CfaN documentary makers – of other miracles occurring when members heard about Ekechukwu's reviving from the dead.**

"A woman who had been on crutches threw them away and started running – and her husband ran to the church altar to ask God to forgive his sins."

According to his own testimony, Daniel Eruchukwu – himself the pastor of the Power Chapel Evangelical Church in Onitsha – was not living right at the time of his accident.

In his interview with CfaN, Erechukwu related that while being rushed to the hospital by ambulance – two angels took him to Heaven. He saw a multitude of people there, dressed in white singing and praising and other scenes too awesome to describe.

Then Daniel says, an angel took him to Hell where he witnessed unspeakable horrors.

The Biblical account of the rich man's plea that Lazarus send someone to warn those who are living, was actually "granted to this generation." The angel then told Daniel Erechukwu that he was being given another chance and "he could return to the living to give "a last warning to this generation."

In a subsequent interview with his good friend Pat Robertson on the 700 Club – Bonnke said, "I didn't know this Pastor Daniel at all. He said the angel told him "if God had not decided to send you back to earth, you would join the people in hell! He was shaking."

Bonnke further relates – "I had him (Daniel Erechukwu) in Vienna. At the same time, while I had my meetings there, there was an esoteric convention there. When they heard that someone had come back from the dead, they love to hear the voices from the dead, and so they said, 'can you not address us?' He went to speak to them, preached, and made an altar call and 50 witches got saved."

Reinhard gave Pat his video "Raised From The Dead" documenting Erechukwu's story. He told Pat, "So many pray for their loved one. This is a step further. This really is a call to salvation that is very urgent."

**With his life-long love for the Lord and a driving passion for the Gospel of Jesus Christ – Reinhard Bonnke has realized in great measure his vision for the continent of Africa. His message remains inclusive. The world is his congregation.**

He and his wife Anni have three children – Kai-Uwe, Gabrielle and Susie. There are eight grandchildren.

Billy Graham and Reinhard Bonnke are admittedly a "tough act to follow." Always standing in the wings waiting their turn however, is the vast convocation of God-called warriors for the souls of men.

As we revisit the lives of those who have gone to their reward – we look back to the memorable ministry of another Billy who left a giant imprint in his own sphere of influence.

# BILLY SUNDAY

### From Baseball to Y.M.C.A.

### To Whirling Dervish

**The heart of God forever broods and yearns over the souls of the men and women, boys and girls whom He created for His glory. He uses the voice of the evangelist to summon them back to the Father's House.**

Many times His call to the work of evangelism is issued in the most unlikely of places and to the most unlikely of persons. Billy Sunday is a case in point.

His entry into the world was inconspicuous to be sure. William Ashley Sunday uttered his first lusty cry in a small, two-room log cabin near Ames, Iowa. America's great Civil War had been in progress for two years, when on November 19th 1862, Billy was born, the third son of William and Mary Jane Corey Sunday.

During the rage of that terrible battle between the States, William Sunday (Billy's father) died of pneumonia. Billy was a mere five weeks old. Even more deaths blighted Billy's early years.

Another body blow to Billy's childhood occurred when his mother placed him (then 12) along with his older brother Edward, in the Soldier's Orphan's Home in Glenwood, Iowa. Undoubtedly this decision was heartbreaking for Mary Jane, but she was so impoverished she could no longer keep their family together.

Now Billy was an "orphan" – a status that often invited peer cruelty. Edward helped Billy to survive. And he developed a love of sports, especially baseball. That God looks after the orphans is a matter of record. James 1: 27

A couple years later Billy and Edward returned to the farm of their Grandfather Corey. Not long afterward however, young Billy, riding a borrowed horse went job hunting in the county seat of Nevada. His work resume would later include jobs of janitor, undertaker's assistant and fireman. He subsequently worked for Iowa's lieutenant governor Colonel John Scott who helped him attend Nevada High School.

Unfortunately, Billy never graduated, but moved to Marshalltown, Iowa where he secured employment in a furniture store. But baseball was Billy's favorite occupation. The town had a team for which he played. Always lightning-quick on his feet, he soon became their star player.

**Unknown to him then, life for Billy Sunday would progress far beyond the ignobility of his poor and parentless roots. In review, it would seem that the game of baseball was the launching pad to the career path God had destined for him.**

A. C. (Pop) Anson who was captain of the Chicago White Stockings "just happened" to be visiting relatives in Marshalltown. While there he 'discovered' the baseball prowess of then twenty-year old Billy. When returned to Chicago Pop Anson sent for Billy.

His successful race against Chicago's crack runner Fred Pfeffer put him ahead by 15 feet and earned Billy a place on that team. Not really adept at batting in the big league, Billy would mostly play center field.

Soon however, his life would take yet another turn. One fateful Sunday in the fall of 1887 – Billy, accompanied by other famous ball players, entered a saloon and got drunk.

Later they sat together on a corner curb, listening to a gospel company across the street who were singing and playing instruments. For Billy it evoked long past memories of his mother singing the same hymns at home and at church.

He began to sob. A young man from the group came over where they were sitting and invited them to come to the Pacific Garden Mission.

In his own words Billy told his comrades, "I'm through. I am going to Jesus Christ. We've come to a parting of the ways." And despite their laughing and mocking – Billy proceeded to the Mission.

That afternoon marked the course of the new Billy Sunday. Falling on his knees he "staggered out of sin and into the arms of the Savior."

Afterward, duly charged by the scripture, "let the redeemed of the Lord say so," Billy testified to his salvation every chance he got, steadily gaining confidence of mind and manner.

He continued to play ball and became widely known as a Christian ballplayer. The YMCA scheduled speaking engagements for him on his baseball circuit. Billy Sunday was soon recognized as a Christian first and a ball player second, and was even appointed by Captain Anson to the position of business manager of the Chicago White Stockings.

Chicago's Jefferson Park Presbyterian Church gained a new member when Billy joined its numbers shortly after his conversion. It was at this church that Billy met and later married the love of his life Helen Amelia Thompson.

Billy had been sold to Pittsburgh with a hefty increase in salary, when on September 5, 1888 their wedding took place in the Thompson home.

Another shot in the arm for Billy was when he was traded in 1897 to Philadelphia. His huge salary was dependent however on his three-year baseball contract that he'd previously signed.

Along with his career Billy had been simultaneously actively engaged in YMCA work. His lucrative compensation as a ball player was a real boon to the family, especially with a baby on the way. Yet Billy was unable to quiet the divine prompting to enter full-time Christian service.

In his spiritual anguish, he put a fleece before God. "Lord, if I can get my release by March 25th, I will go into YMCA work. If I don't get it, I will accept that as evidence you want me to continue playing ball, an I will play out the rest of my contract." The Philadelphia league finally notified Billy of his release. It was March 17th. **When God speaks – other voices must take a backseat.**

But leagues were reluctant to give up such a prize player as Billy. Soon he was offered another contract, this time with Cincinnati. It was for a whopping $5,000 dollars – for just one season!

Because of the then prevalent "hard times," Billy had almost stilled his conscience to accept his latest offer. But faithful Helen, his wife rebuked him. "You promised God" she told him, "you promised God that you would quit. Stick to your promise."

With her words ringing in his ears, Billy said yes to the YMCA program. He conducted street meetings. He distributed literature and was active in fund raising projects. Routine office duties and securing speakers for their noon prayer meetings were also part of the deal. And that deal paid him only $83.00 a month. Quite a comedown from $5,000, but with his wife's encouragement he stayed the course.

It was 1893 and the next step on God's agenda was Billy's connection to the team of J. Wilbur Chapman. Serving as general helper and advance man, he became familiar with all phases of evangelism.

Then unexpectedly, Billy's world would be rocked again. Following a sudden decision, Chapman, his mentor, returned to the pastorate. It was Christmas Eve 1895.

Now what?

The Sundays, though initially shocked at the evangelist's abrupt departure – would not be left high and dry. A letter of far-reaching importance arrived a few days later. The writer was a Presbyterian pastor in Garner, Iowa.

The pastor advised Billy that he would be uniting with Baptist and Methodist ministers to hold a city-wide revival in Garner at a rented opera house. His message further read: "We would like to know if you would be our evangelist and lead us in the revival. Let us know at once please."

Gladly accepting the honor afforded him, Billy went to Garner with 8 of Chapman's sermons. The Lord blessed. From January 8th through the 17th 1896, 268 souls were saved. And the rest is history.

The Presbyterian Church awarded Billy Sunday his license to preach in 1898. And in 1903 he was ordained.

Then came the crusades, nearly fifty of them. From January of 1902 until December of 1910 – crusades were held in predominately in small mid-western towns in Iowa, Illinois, Missouri, Minnesota, Colorado, Pennsylvania, Washington and Ohio.

Low, straight roofs took the place of lofty ceilings in many of his tabernacles that had no balconies. His speaker's platform was invariably placed as far to the center as possible. Behind the platform names of converts were recorded and daily sent to city pastors. Everything was maintained fireproof.

**The Portsmouth, Ohio campaign that began the last Sunday of 1910 was six weeks long and ended in February 1911 bringing 5,200 converts. Then came Lima, Ohio and 5,700 converts. Surpassing all the others, the Toledo crusade generated 7,300**

**converts and brought Billy Sunday to national attention.**

Sunday's amazingly fruitful crusades continued. One standout crusade in 1912 brought 25% of the population of Wilkes-Barre, Pennsylvania to faith in Jesus Christ. Two hundred of the city's taverns were reputedly closed as a result. The September/October crusade in Steubenville, Ohio in 1913 reportedly drew one third of that city to the Savior.

The crusades proceed to bigger cities. And Sunday's remarkable harvest of souls increases accordingly.

**What was Evangelist Billy Sunday like?** For starters he stood adamantly against what he considered the degrading social practices of the day – alluring female fashions, movies, playing cards – and the most odious of all – the demon booze. His fiery denunciation of drinking was obviously instrumental in Prohibition being passed.

Sunday didn't back away from other social issues of his time either. He addressed women's suffrage, child labor, segregation and a host of additional hot topics.

His pulpit manner was frequently criticized (even by some Christian leaders) as unorthodox. In one newspaper account, Sunday was described as a "whirling dervish." But his sermons were down to earth and practical and replete with illustrations.

Billy's stock of words was decidedly rough. To justify himself, Sunday would say, "I want to preach the gospel so plainly that men can come from the factories and not have to bring a dictionary."

Though not in the approved platform style of his predecessors, Sunday's antics more than thrilled his audiences who kept coming and making decisions for the Lord.

He never compromised the message. If his words were burning, cutting and offensive – they were purposefully calculated to conquer the hearts of men for the Christ of Calvary,

What powered this intensity of desire to win souls for Jesus Christ? What was the single most motivating factor that propelled Billy Sunday to so ardently pour his whole self into his preaching – night or day, year after year?

**What supernatural enabling rested on his ministry that drew untold thousands to submit their lives to the ownership of the Master? Without question it was the Holy Spirit! Billy Sunday was anointed with Spirit fire.**

**No human attribute – whether of wisdom, learning or charismatic fervor can birth a single soul's salvation. Only the convicting power of the Spirit of God can accomplish that.**

Billy Sunday credited J. Wilbur Chapman and his three-year apprenticeship under Chapman's ministry, with the molding of his own doctrine on the fullness of the Holy Spirit. He preached about Holy Ghost power and considered it absolutely necessary for soul winning.

And Billy was convinced that he dare not trifle with this sacred anointing – that he was supremely obligated to please God rather than men.

It was further apparent to his constituents that Billy Sunday had met the conditions of the Holy Spirit's in-filling – for its power was amply evident throughout his ministry.

Every occasion when Billy preached – without exception – his Bible lay open to Isaiah 61:1 with his sermon notes laid upon these words:

**"The Spirit of the Lord is upon me; because the Lord has anointed me to preach good tidings unto the meek; He has sent me to bind up the broken-hearted, to proclaim liberty to the captives and the opening of the prisons to them that are bound."**

Did those words for Billy Sunday represent his own experience with God? It was abundantly evident that time after anointed time he preached without compromise, *"not regarding the faces of men"* with an infusion of power that was clearly not of this world.

**Incidentally that very verse in Isaiah was the same one that Jesus read in the synagogue in…announcing afterward declaring, *"this day is this scripture fulfilled in your ears."***

Luke 4: 21

In a real way, Billy Sunday was his own person, unique and definitely not a copy. His preaching style took him back and forth over the platform with all kinds of gesturing. His hour-long sermons were calculated to bring in a harvest of souls. His prayer life was "without ceasing."

Billy was a hand-shaker – with everyone who came forward. The offering on the last day of any crusade was given to him and that offering only.

Regrettably, his relationships with his daughter and three sons were not as close as he would have liked and all four died at an early age. As his business manager, his wife Helen was his right arm and a trusted confidant.

**It is estimated that in the course of his ministry Billy Sunday preached to millions and reaped a harvest of some 300,000 souls for Jesus Christ. He had turned his back on a lucrative baseball career, preferring instead to pour out his life in service for the Master.**

As a staunch Bible believer, undoubtedly he looked forward to the day when the Lord would say to him: *"Well done, good and faithful servant … enter into the joy of your Lord."* Matthew 25: 21

**Billy Sunday was called home on November 6, 1935 just 13 days before his 73rd birthday.** Funeral services were held at

Moody Memorial Church in Chicago with Pastor Harry Ironside officiating.

Pastor Ironside related the story of Billy's conversion followed by his eulogy. Billy's song-leader and choir director, Homer Rodeheaver and team member Harry Clarke also gave tributes. Renowned Presbyterian pastor John Timothy Stone spoke eloquently. In a fitting conclusion, the congregation sang

"O That Will be Glory for Me."

# DWIGHT LYMAN MOODY

**Born February 5, 1837**

**Died December 1899**

**His Methods of Children's Ministry**

**Earned Him the Nickname of "Crazy Moody"**

Dwight Lyman Moody was the sixth of nine children born to Edwin and Betsy Moody in Northfield Massachasetts. Only four years later when his mother Betsy was pregnant with their twins, tragically his father collapsed and died right in front of her. His parents had not previously known the gravity of his physical condition.

Now fatherless at age ten, Dwight's formal education ended and he was expected to work from then on to support himself.

Young Dwight was seventeen when in April of 1854 he sought greater job opportunities in the much larger city of Boston. Fortunately for Dwight, his uncles Samuel and Lemuel Holten operated prosperous retail shoe and boot stores in Boston and he became his Uncle Samuel's top salesman, and afterward conscientiously provided shoes for his mother and siblings. Dwight began attending the local Mount Vernon Congregational Church.

A devout middle-aged man, Edward Kimball was Dwight's Sunday School Class leader. Led of the Lord he took personal interest in eighteen year old Dwight's spiritual state. Recalling Mr. Kimball's impromptu visit to the shoe store that Saturday in 1855, Dwight said:

"I had not felt that I had a soul till then. I said to myself, 'This is a very strange thing. Here is a man who never saw me till lately, and he is weeping over my sins, and I never shed a tear about them.' But I understand it now, and know what it is to have a passion for men's souls and weep over their sins. I don't remember what he said, but I can feel the power of that man's hand on my shoulder. It was not long after that I was brought into the Kingdom of God."

He remembers how Christ made everything different for him from then on. The sun shone brighter. Birds in the trees seemed to be singing their songs especially for him. "It seemed to me that I was in love with all creation. I had not a bitter feeling against any man, and I was ready to take all men to my heart. If a man has not the love of God shed abroad in his heart, he has never been regenerated."

Feeling a lack of accomplishment, Dwight later headed for Chicago in search of a cause he could champion, and there renewed his affiliation with the Young Men's Christian Association.

Although Sunday Schools and Missions were plentiful in Chicago, orphaned children and children living in impoverished homes or those adversely affected by alcoholism were not being reached. He would reach them.

Already a successful shoe salesman in Chicago, Dwight rented a vacant saloon and set it up as an independent "Sabbath School." It was in the heart of Chicago's worst slum – 'The Sands' being an area known as "Little Hell."

**In the barest of surroundings, with an old barrel as his pulpit Dwight taught a growing number of children who sat on the floor – enticing them to come with maple sugar candy and pennies. For this he was nicknamed "Crazy Moody" – but these children became his passion and by 1860 his Sabbath Schools had grown to some 1,500 weekly participants.**

**In November of that year, the successful ministry work of**

**Dwight Lyman Moody – would receive recognition from Pres-
ident-elect Abraham Lincoln, who paid a visit to his school.**
Months later, seventy-five of those who heard Lincoln speak responded to his call for volunteers and enlisted to save the Union.

During the War Between the States, Dwight felt God was leading him into full-time ministry. He gave up his business career.
Still working for the YMCA, he served as president of the Chicago
branch for three years. The experience would prepare him for his
upcoming revival ministry.

Meanwhile, the country was embroiled in battles about Abraham
Lincoln's platform of preventing any new territories becoming
slave states. Prior to Lincoln's taking office, seven states seceded
from the Union with four more states withdrawing after his inau-
guration. A diplomatic settlement was out of the question after the
newly created Confederacy fired on Fort Sumter on April 12, 1861.

New recruits soon filled Camp Douglas, three miles north of Chicago. The YMCA engaged in ministry to the spiritual needs of
these soldiers. Dwight, B. F. Jacobs and John Farwell were placed
in charge of these efforts. Moody conducted eight, sometimes ten
services a day. The Association distributed thousands of tracts.
Other religious materials were also handed out. Hundreds of conversions resulted, as well as countless re-dedications to Christ.

When the YMCA formed a Christian Commission to better minister to the soldiers, Dwight was chosen as their Chicago delegate.
Nine times Dwight would travel with General Ulysses S. Grant's
forces to the front lines. When Richmond fell to the Union, Dwight
was one of the first Northerners to enter that city.

He and Emma would marry on August 28, 1862 and have their
daughter Emma (named for her mother and grandmother) on October 24, 1864.

Three years later the Moodys would journey to England, for Emma's health and to meet with the YMCA's London founder and establish important contacts with English evangelists.

Dwight's formal career as a revivalist began in 1872 in Great Britain. The famous Ira David Sankey became his singing partner and accompanied him in all his major revivals. They achieved widespread support in Scotland before conducting a long series of campaigns in England.

Moody had become a national figure. When he returned to America in 1875, he launched a series of huge revival meetings in Chicago, Philadelphia, New York and Boston.

Harry Moorhouse whom he'd met when he went to Great Britain, deeply influenced Moody with his powerful messages on the love of God. Yet his life and ministry would be even more transformed with his baptism in the Holy Spirit.

Dwight remembered his former encounters – first with an old man who had told him at a Sabbath School meeting, "Young man when you speak again honor the Holy Ghost." He recalled subsequent encounters with two women who were praying for him and years later praying with him on Friday afternoons in a YMCA building to receive the Holy Ghost and fire.

**Meeting after meeting, Dwight would agonize before the Lord – crying and pleading with God for the baptism. In 1871 his prayer would be answered in an unusual way.** Prior to a return trip to England, he was planning, Dwight was walking up Wall Street in New York when suddenly the power of God fell upon him. Hurrying to the house of a friend, he stayed in a room by himself for hours as the Holy Ghost filled his soul with such joy he had to ask God to stay his hand or he'd die.

Back in London in June of 1872 an anointed Dwight Moody spoke at Reverend John Lessey's church and that night nearly all the congregation responded to his invitation to be saved.

Work in York began slowly but mushroomed as the local pastors supported the evangelist. The Brits were accustomed to sermons that were more like lectures but welcomed Dwight's up front confident preaching. One Briton described his delivery this way:

"He is a master in his work; he aims at one thing, viz; getting people to consider their state before God, and he brings everything to bear on the one object – to accept Jesus, as offered to us in the Gospel. From this aim he is never for a moment diverted."

"His simplest illustrations; his most touching stories; his most pathetic appeals; his gentlest persuasiveness; his most passionate declamation; his most direct home thrusts; his (almost unfair) reference to people and places; all are used, and unsparingly, unfearingly used, for the one purpose of touching the heart – that Jesus and the Father may come in and abide there."

Some two hundred people joined the churches in York alone. Speaking in a public hall (not wishing to favor any denomination) at the invitation of Baptist Pastor Arthur A. Rees in Sunderland resulted in overflowing churches. Continuing the meetings for two more years, they went on to Scotland and Ireland, returning to England in November of 1874 to continue the campaign. July 12, 1875 would be their last service. Dwight and singer-parter Ira Sankey would conduct 285 meetings, addressing 2,500,000 souls in London alone, before returning to the work in America.

Evangelist Moody relied heavily on his enduement of Spirit power. As he became more prominent, his influence spread. He fervently preached the Baptism of the Holy Ghost as a second gift following salvation. And he urged Dr. Torrey and others to preach it also.

**Moody said: "We must pray for the Holy Spirit for service; that we may be anointed and qualified to do the work God has for us to do."**

He further emphasized the importance of the anointing in his sermon on "Hindered Power." Strongly expressing his conviction he said: "I have lived long enough to know that if I cannot have the power of the Spirit of God on me to help me to work for Him, I would rather die, than to live just for the sake of living."

Missionary-Evangelist Dwight Lyman Moody – founded Moody Church and before his death in 1899 – founded the Moody Bible Institute both in Chicago. His legacy remains to this day.

# JOHN BENJAMIN WESLEY

## (LITTLE JACKIE)

### "A Brand Plucked From the Burning"

### Born June 1703 – Died March 1791

The story of this renowned English religious trailblazer is unique among revivalists. John Wesley's fervent Christ-centered leadership ultimately revolutionized the Church of England. The Anglican Church of his time had lost its passion. The urgent spiritual needs of the masses were being neglected – in the wake of the prevailing ignorance, political maneuverings and the influences of rationalism and deism.

Thanks to the untiring efforts of John Wesley and his brother Charles – not only England would be spiritually rejuvenated, but the far regions of Continental Europe and America would also be greatly influenced.

Rev. Samuel Wesley, an Anglican minister and his wife Susanna enhanced their pastorate with a devoted and uncompromising Christian morality. John was the fifteenth of their 19 children of whom only 10 reached adulthood. He was born on June 17, 1703 in the Epworth parsonage in Lincolnshire.

The Wesley children were reared in a quietly strict disciplined environment reinforced by daily exercise of prayer, study and manners. This early background would serve John well in his search for God.

Tragedy would strike the Wesley household as they slept on the night of February 9, 1709. The Epworth parsonage caught fire (no one knew the source) sometime after eleven and the family was driven outside without clothes or possessions.

Adding to their concern, Susanna was close to delivering her last child and she did suffer burns making sure everyone got out safely. Only one was missing – five year old Jackie.

Despite Samuel's attempts to reenter the house, the intensity of the flames prevented him. Fortunately a neighbor had rescued the child from a second story room. Minutes later the entire rectory was reduced to rubble.

**Little John was quite literally "a brand plucked from the burning," as his father was wont to say. And ever afterward his mother Susanna firmly believed (what was to be amply proven) that John was especially called of God.**

Following preliminary studies at Charterhouse School, John at age 17 enrolled in Christ Church Oxford, earning a Bachelor of Arts degree in 1724. A year later he was ordained a deacon in the Church of England.

Lincoln College Oxford elected John Wesley a fellow in 1726 and the following year he became curate (assistant) to his father. After his ordination as a priest in 1728, he resumed the duties of his fellowship at Lincoln. He then joined what was derisively called "the Holy Club" – a religious society that his younger brother Charles espoused.

Besides study, discussion, prayer and church services – members of the Holy Club were generous with their donations to the needy. They also ministered to the orphaned and destitute and visited prisoners.

The young popular preacher George Whitefield was one of this 25-member group. Later in America Whitefield would give impetus to **the Great Awakening** – boosting it into a vigorous driving force not only religiously, but politically and socially as well.

After their father's death in 1735, the Wesley brothers accompanied Colonel James Oglethorpe (a former friend of Samuel Wesley) to Savannah, Georgia to minister to settlement of about 520 people. John was appointed chaplain and the newly ordained Charles his secretary.

Two years after their return to London, the Wesley brothers hosted a "love feast" with George Whitefield and Benjamin Ingham (a fellow missionary to Georgia) and 58 others.

As the midnight hour struck they all prayed and praised until 3 that morning. Then, overpowered by the Spirit of the Lord, these worshippers fell to the ground. In his journal Whitefield later wrote:

**"It was a Pentecost season indeed: Entire nights were spent in prayer. Often have we been filled as with new wine; and often have I seen them overwhelmed with the Divine Presence, and cry out, "Will God indeed dwell with men upon the earth?" How dreadful is this place? This is no other than the house of God and the gate of heaven!"**

"Salvation is free to all" – the heart of John's preaching – was offensive to many clergy of the Calvinistic Church of England and they denied him their pulpits. Urged by Whitefield, John Wesley took his message outside the church doors. His first open air sermon was preach on a little hill near Bristol. Biographer Basil Miller described it this way:

"Here was a crowd of people" (some 3,000) "to whom his message would come as a bursting light from heaven, and he would not deny them this glimpse of Christ."

Despite the evangelistic fervor and the enthusiastic response of the masses to the Wesleys' message of salvation – with its corresponding moral disciplined life – doctrinal differences inevitably arose.

This wonderful stirring of God had been bearing much fruit. But sadly, because of divisive theological dogmas, three distinctly different movements would evolve – Whitefield's "Calvinistic Methodism", Moravianism and the Wesleyan "United Societies."

For the edification of these Societies, somewhat patterned after the monastic orders of Roman Catholism – John Wesley wrote numerous theological works. He also edited 35 volumes of Christian literature.

**So intent was John Wesley on spreading the Gospel of Jesus Christ beyond the confines of the established English church – he covered more than 250,000 miles on horseback the length and breadth of England. During his career he preached over 40,000 sermons.**

His credo is summed up in his own words:

"I look upon all the world as my parish; thus far I mean, that in whatever part of it I am, I judge it meet, right and my bounden duty to declare unto all that are willing to hear, the glad tidings of salvation."

Conservative in dress, John Wesley was slight of build and small in stature. Yet he had a commanding presence and was portrayed by many as a spiritual giant.

Always loyal, but disappointed in the apparent disinterest and opposition of the Anglican Church, Wesley secured the legal standing if the Methodist Society by taking out a deed of declaration in 1784. Also that year he ordained two "superintendents" for Methodists in North America.

**Married to Molly Vazeille for 30 years (she died in 1781) they had no children. John preached his final sermon "Seek ye the Lord while He may be found" – on February 23, 1791. Three days later on March 2nd, surround by his loved ones, John Wesley went to be with the Lord Jesus.**

# CHARLES WESLEY

### *A Brother and a Helper*

### Born December 18, 1707

### Died March 29, 1788

It is only fitting to acknowledge the great role Charles Wesley played as confidante and closest associate to his brother John.

**Charles Wesley was also an ordained Anglican priest and for 50 years along with his brother, preached a like message of faith and salvation.**

A brilliant scholar and master of the English language – Charles wrote some 6,500 hymns including "Hark The Herald Angels Sing" and "Jesus Lover of my Soul" which are still an ongoing blessing to the Christian world. Charles died at age 81 in London.

The Methodist Church enjoys a wonderful heritage in the Wesley brothers.

# PETER CARTWRIGHT

**Circuit Riding Preacher at 18!**

**Born September 1, 1785**

**Died September 25, 1872**

The American frontier and the Methodist Episcopal Church were the twin settings shaping the life of Peter Cartwright.

Born in a cluster of cane trees to the yet unwed Christiana Garvin, as she hid from attacking Indians – Peter was the son of Revolutionary War veteran Peter Cartwright Sr., who later married his mother.

The family moved from Amhurst County, Virginia to then opening up Kentucky territory – when Peter was five. Their homestead was north of the Kentucky/Tennessee border in Russellville, the county seat.

His mother joined the church and tried earnestly to mold young Peter into a Christian lifestyle. His father's influence was at times much stronger than his praying mother. He actually condoned Peter's passion for dancing, card-playing, gambling (an addiction) and horseracing – buying him his own fine racing horse. Peter was by his own admission – a "naturally wild, wicked boy."

At 16 however, his behavior was to change dramatically, when feeling tremendous guilt – he told his father to sell his horse, allowed his mother to burn his cards in the fire – and regularly read the Testament and began fasting and praying.

That spring, a minister of the Presbyterian Church (Mr. McGready) held a sacramental congregational meeting at the Red River Meeting House nearby. Already under extreme conviction Peter attended the all night gathering and with a number of others – all weeping – went forward and begged God for mercy. Describing his agony of soul, he related what happened next:

**"An impression was made on my mind, as though a voice said to me *"Thy sins are all forgiven thee."* He continued: "Divine light flashed all around me, unspeakable joy sprung up in my soul. I rose to my feet, opened my eyes, and it really seemed a if I was in heaven; the trees, the leaves on them, and everything seemed, and I really thought were, praising God." Eighty seekers found their peace with God that night.**

The Communion season began the following year with Peter's pastor recognizing him as an "exhorter" for the Methodists and he became at only 18, a regular circuit rider. Peter traveled with another minister for three months and the Lord confirmed his calling with the addition of 26 conversions.

During a funeral service Peter performed in a Baptist meeting house the Holy Spirit again manifested and 23 souls were saved.

Peter was ordained in 1806 by Francis Asbury at the Western Conference. Now a deacon in the Methodist Episcopal Church he was sent to serve at the Ohio Border where he encountered the conflicting sects of Unitarianism, Univeralism, Deism and others.

In that diverse climate, Peter would sharpen his reasoning powers and hone his skill as a debater. Peter was subsequently assigned a circuit in the Cumberland district of Chillicothe, Ohio. There he met and married Frances Gaines, thus breaking the tradition of celibacy.

The Western Conference began October 1, 1808 in Liberty Hill, Tennessee near Nashville. Before its end Bishop McKendree made Peter an elder in the Methodist Church. He was later to be elected twelve times to the General Conference.

The Cartwrights had seven children while living in Kentucky. In 1824 when their eldest daughter Eliza reached fourteen, the family pulled up stakes and moved to an Illinois farm.

**Peter Cartwright's eloquent preaching profoundly moved his audiences, as in the case of one camp meeting in the 1830's – when 500 of his listeners fell on their knees to seek the Lord. During that two-week meeting over a thousand souls were added to the church.**

At 39, Peter had earned the reputation of being a formidable preacher and prominent public figure. As presiding elder he continued his circuit duties while still managing his farm.

**Additionally Peter became active in the politics of the day – running for a seat in the General Assembly of the Illinois Legislature. He won his seat in 1828 and again in 1832 over his opponent Abraham Lincoln.**

Slavery had become a highly controversial issue causing division even among the church membership. Peter Cartwright would take a strong stand against it.

His Autobiography would state his views this way:

"Slavery had long been agitated in the Methodist Episcopal Church. Our preachers, did not feel it their duty to meddle with it politically, yet, as Christians and Christian ministers, to their eternal credit, they believed it to be their duty to bear their testimony against slavery as a moral evil. And this is the reason why the General Conference, from time to time, passed rules and regulations to govern preachers and members of the Church in regard to this great evil."

"The great object of the General Conference was to keep the ministry clear of it. And there can be no doubt that the course pursued by early Methodist preachers was the cause of the emancipation of thousands of this degraded race of human beings."

"It is clear to my mind, if Methodist preachers had kept clear of slavery themselves and gone on bearing honest testimony against it, that thousands upon thousands more would have been emancipated who are now groaning under oppression too intolerable to be borne. Slavery is certainly a domestic, political and moral evil."

Again in 1846, Cartwright and Lincoln competed for a U. S. Senate seat. This time Lincoln defeated Cartwright by a whopping 1,500 votes.

**It is said that Cartwright a tall, burly and purposeful carrier of the Gospel, was largely responsible for the rapid growth of Methodism in the Ohio River and Mississippi River valleys."**

His best-selling book "Autobiography of Peter Cartwright – The Backwoods Preacher" (edited by W. P. Strickland and released in 1856) chronicled his colorful career and detailed often humorous glimpses of pioneer church life. Peter wrote "Fifty Years As a Presiding Elder" in 1871 among his other works.

Peter Cartwright retired in 1869. He had barely turned 87 when he passed away on September 25, 1872.

**Thank God for the parade of stalwart men and women whose lives were poured out (as incense) in the evangelistic service of the Master. May their number ever increase. How tirelessly, how steadfastly these dynamic emissaries of the Lord wooed the masses with the saving Gospel of the Kingdom.**

Before He ascended to the Father, Jesus promised the enabling power of the Spirit to His assembled disciples.

***"You shall receive power when the Holy Ghost is come upon you and you shall be witnesses unto Me in Jerusalem, and in all Judea and Samaria, and unto the uttermost part of the earth." –***

**Acts 1:8. And the second chapter of Acts confirms the Lord's prophecy.**

Although they lived at different times and labored for the Gospel in different areas – it would appear that these great **"witnesses"** to the Lord they served – all shared a common denominator.

**The power that characterized their ministries was the unmistakable anointing of the Holy Ghost. For each of them the in-filling of the Spirit was an exciting confirmation of their calling.**

Records show however, that not all spoke with other tongues. Yet the undeniable power of the Holy Ghost was amply evident in their ministries – as they moved countless thousands to embrace salvation in Jesus Christ.

# EVAN ROBERTS

Welsh Evangelist Evan (Ivan) Roberts testified that he earnestly sought the Spirit for 13 years. Then at one morning meeting his prayers were answered.

Upon hearing an evangelist pray similarly, Evan pleaded with God - "O Lord bend me, bend me!" On his knees he agonized with sweat and overflowing tears, which felt to him like blood pouring out.

**Describing what happened, Roberts recounted: "I felt a living force coming into my bosom. This grew and grew, and I was almost bursting. My bosom was boiling." Friends later said it was then that the glory broke. Whereupon an overwhelming peace filled him and he was thus made ready for the mighty revival that came as the fullness of the Spirit shaped him into a great soul winner.**

# D. L. MOODY

His personal experience with the Holy Spirit (mentioned elsewhere) prompted **D. L. Moody** to insist thereafter that **the Baptism** was a distinctly separate gift.

**He came to accept that following conversion the Holy Spirit does dwell with every believer.** *"He that dwelleth with you shall be in you."* **John 14: 17. However, Moody also believed every Christian should seek the baptism of the Holy Spirit.**

"We have to ask for this blessing, to knock for it, to seek for it…" And Moody avidly sought to keep the power of the Spirit of God upon him! Reiterating his stirring words in "Hindered Power" – Moody said of the anointing:

**"I have lived long enough to know that if I cannot have the power of the Spirit of God on me to help me to work for Him, I would rather die, than to live just for the sake of living."**

References: Moody, His Words, Work and Workers –

Edited by Rev. W. H. Daniels

The Life of D. L. Moody by his son.

# EVANGELIST JOHN R. RICE

During the years of his service for the Lord – **Evangelist John R. Rice** (1895-1980) carefully observed the many different reactions of people to their salvation experiences and subsequent Holy Spirit fillings.

Evangelist Rice commented: "It is not wise to base a doctrine on human experience. The greatest soul winners verify the clear statements of Jesus Christ in Acts 1:8.

# R. A. TORREY

**Dr. Torrey was a soul-winning powerhouse.** Considered Moody's most trusted helper and later his successor, the anointing of the Holy Ghost definitely attended his ministry. During a world-wide tour, Dr. Torrey's campaigns reported a record hundred thousand souls saved.

Describing the work of the Spirit in his book – **The Holy Spirit: Who He is, and What He does** – Dr. Torrey makes three definitive statements:

1. In the first place, the Baptism of the Holy Spirit is a definite experience of which one may know whether he has received it or not....

2. In the second place, the Baptism of the Holy Spirit is a work of the Holy Spirit distinct from and additional to His regenerating work....

3. In the third place, the Baptism with the Holy Spirit is a work of the Holy Spirit always connected with and primarily for the purpose of testimony and service.

**We might add that this blessing for service is the special empowerment of God, not only fitting Christians to win souls, but also enabling us to live holy lives.**

# CHARLES G. FINNEY

### Converted and Baptized with the Holy Spirit

### The Same Day!

A mighty revivalist Charles G. Finney manifested the power of God to such a degree, that multiplied thousands were drawn to the Lord. Seeing souls saved was the high point of Finney's ministry and he pursued his calling with great intensity.

In his own **Autobiography of Charles G. Finney,** he tells about how he received the fullness of the Holy Spirit. Finney is also quoted by Dr. Oswald J. Smith in **The Revival We Need** where he states:

"I was powerfully converted on the morning of the month of October, 1822. In the evening of the same day I received overwhelming baptisms of the Holy Ghost, that went through me, as it seemed to me – body and soul. I immediately found myself endued with such power from on high that a few words dropped here and there to individuals were the means of their immediate conversion."

**Attributing the baptism of the Spirit and subsequent in-fillings, to prayer and more often to prayer coupled with fasting, this mighty soul winner said: "This has been the experience of my life."**

Although he had not sought or expected a particular feeling – Finney experienced a wonderful sense of God's presence upon him. And the power of the Holy Spirit manifested itself in all his teaching and practice.

# J. WILBUR CHAPMAN

The Holy Ghost became real to Dr. Wilbur Chapman as he consecrated himself before God and by faith claimed from the Father – the fullness of the Spirit. His life changed from that moment on as the reality of the in-filling of the Holy Ghost touched every area of his life – family, Bible study, preaching. **For Dr. Chapman the scripture,** *"Old things have passed away – Behold all things become new"* **– became the driving reality of his life.**

Chapman moved hearts. In the power of the Holy Spirit Chapman led many souls to Jesus. Formerly experiencing salvation through the mentoring of Moody – J. Wilbur Chapman became the vice-president of Moody Bible Institute.

He also authored the book, **The Life and Work of D. L. Moody.**

**That God breathed upon these men who devoted themselves to harvesting souls for the Kingdom – is amply evident in their ministries. Holy Ghost power is available for all Christians as they humble themselves, surrender to Christ and ask Him. Powerful soul winners who we've mentioned thus far – though distanced from one another – were in concord and with one voice – declared with surety that they were filled with the Holy Spirit. And their ministries bore much fruit. Such a one was the great preacher Charles Haddon Spurgeon.**

# CHARLES HADDON SPURGEON

**1834-1892**

**CHARLES HADDON SPURGEON** was a mighty Spirit-filled messenger of God. This highly esteemed Englishman devoted his forty years of ministry (three times a week) to Kingdom building.

**Born in Kelvedon, Essex – at only twenty years old, he became (in 1854) pastor of the New Park Street Chapel in London.** Within five years his congregation had grown so large that the Metropolitan Tabernacle was erected for him – this facility seating 6,000 people.

Scorning liberalism in the church, Spurgeon relied on the Scriptures for instruction and direction. Conscious always of a powerful anointing of the Holy Spirit, he led hundreds of thousands to faith in Christ. Some thought him to be the greatest preacher since the Apostle Paul.

**In his book entitled Twelve Sermons on the Holy Spirit Spurgeon underscored <u>the outpouring, the indwelling and the overflowing of the Holy Spirit.</u> Recalling from scripture that *"Jesus of Nazareth was anointed of the Holy Spirit,"* he proclaimed to his audiences – "If Jesus Christ, the great founder of our religion needed to be anointed of the Holy Spirit, how much more our ministers?**

Spurgeon emphasized further in the same book, that **prayer was key** to receiving the Holy Spirit, citing several Bible verses supporting the need to specifically ask for God's promises!

**"Ask God to make you all that the Spirit of God can make you!"**

Charles Haddon Spurgeon left an awesome legacy of souls won to the Lord. And a life spent in the power of His presence. He authored 50 volumes of popular sermons, plus a number of other works.

# MORE SPIRIT-FILLED GIANTS

In his book **The Rest of Faith Rev. A. B. Earle, D.D.** highlights his experiences in ministry beginning in 1830. That he had a special enduement of power was amply evident. A Baptist evangelist, Earle testified that it was through the Holy Ghost that he was enabled to win 157,000 souls to Jesus Christ.

**Dr. A. T. Pierson** had preached for some eighteen years, relying on skilled oratory, literary understanding and an affinity for the culture. However, according to his own testimony to other ministers (recorded in **Holiness and Power by Hills)** Dr. Pierson related how his ministry was dramatically changed after he had received holiness and power through the baptism of the Holy Spirit.

Said Dr. Pierson: "Brethren, I have seen more conversions and accomplished more in the eighteen months sine I received that blessing than in the eighteen years previous."

**Only Heaven will reveal the number of men and women trail-blazers, who under the anointing of the Spirit – garnered a veritable host of souls to be added to the Lamb's Book of Life.**

Among them were, **"Praying Hyde"** missionary and revivalist to India, whose anointing also won thousands. And **Dr. L. R. Scarborough,** teacher and president of the Southwestern Baptist Theological Seminary, whose Spirit-filled ministry led some twenty thousand to the saving Christ. After receiving the power of God, **Len G. Broughton** greatly increased his soul- winning ministry – baptizing three hundred that same year.

These mighty soul-winners did not claim to speak in tongues. But all embraced the fullness of the Holy Spirit – the power of Pentecost. Each had a definite experience that ultimately changed the course of their ministry.

**Essentially, they all believed that Holy Ghost anointing – the enduement of the power of Pentecost – came in response to prevailing prayer. To diminish the need for Holy Spirit power for soul winning is to depart from the stirring up of revival. Jesus himself stressed its absolute necessity.**

# THE AWESOME MOVE OF
# THE SPIRIT

**Beginning at the dawn of the 20ᵗʰ century – the Christian faith received an awesome outpouring of God's supernatural adrenaline.**

The Welsh revival in 1904 sparked a worldwide reawakening. It ultimately generated the significant and long lasting Azusa Street revival in Los Angeles.

There had been in this city a decline in trust. Disinterest and apathy had taken over. Believer and unbeliever alike were questioning the authenticity of God's sovereignty over history and the relevance of Scriptural authority. "Show me" cried Los Angeles!

And our all-knowing God showed them! He used a humble black man who waited expectantly while his heart listened intently. His name was **William J. Seymour.** In a small nondescript building on Azusa Street – God Almighty demonstrated His awesome power with reverberations that were heard around the country!

Begun with fervent cottage prayer meetings the ensuing revival drew countless souls who were touched forever. Sinfulness exposed resulted in sins forgiven. Disbelief and destructive habits, bondage and broken-ness, moral decline and shallow spirituality were systematically routed. Genuine salvation and a hunger for righteous living followed the Divine makeover.

**Miracles occurred. Healing – emotional and physical – was attributed to the nearness of the healing Jesus. Fire from heaven fell with suddenness. Prayer was pungent and penetrating. The Lord by his Holy Spirit revealed himself and the treasures of His love and mercy.**

## ENEMY ONSLAUGHT

Unfortunately, people in the professions who embraced the biblical reports of the miraculous and personally participated – were often excluded from mainstream society, and sadly even within their denominational ranks.

**The concept of the Holy Scriptures being taken at face value – was soundly rejected by the intelligentsia.**

Opposition notwithstanding, the fires of Christian revival spread. New believers multiplied. Curiosity seekers came to observe the strange "goings on" and met **The Master!** Backsliders returned to their "first love." Transformation – spiritual, emotional, mental and physical took place as the people – hungry for the reality of God – believed.

# FIRES OF AZUSA STREET STILL BURN

## REVIVAL SPREADS

**The legacy of Azusa Street – where the power of Pentecost was reintroduced continues to this day.** Winds of the Spirit blew mightily throughout the 20<sup>th</sup> century. Into this arena of spiritual awakening emerged great and renowned soul-winners – and the less prominent, but effective soldiers of the Great Commission.

## EARLY PENTECOSTAL FIREBRANDS

**Aimee Semple McPherson** was a prominent figure in the early Pentecostal Movement of Canada. With her husband Robert they traveled to Hong Kong as missionaries. Aimee was the founder of the International Church of the Four Square Gospel.

**Maria B. Woodworth-Etter** let nothing stop her vibrant witness. Despite her extreme ill health – sometimes she needed to be carried to the platform – Mrs. Woodworth-Etter ministered in a powerful anointing.

Many healing miracles attended her meetings – as well as supernatural manifestations of a heavenly choir. She too founded a church that she pastored until 1924 when she died after 50 years of ministry.

**Smith Wigglesworth** from Brandford, England gained world renown as an evangelist and apostle commanding large audiences under a heavy anointing.

**This sovereign move of God accompanied by the fullness of the Spirit with signs following – crossed denominational lines and continued to spread around the country and beyond.**

# THE INTERSECTING GOD

**In every generation since the Garden of Eden, our Creator has endeavored to reconnect and reconcile with His creation.**

**The visitation of God in the Twentieth Century** and prior – spread the transforming message of **Jesus** – in America and worldwide. Many re-awakenings were spawned. Against the turbulent backdrop of World Wars I and II, natural disasters and moral decline – these major revivals ignited the flames of renewal. And without a doubt – **God showed up!**

**Author and Church historian, Richard Riss chronicles the highlights of a significant of number spiritual awakenings – in his book "A Survey of 20th Century Revival Movements in North America."**

**Among others he mentions were the Healing, Latter Rain and Pentecostal Movements; the Catholic Charismatic Movement; the Jesus Movement and Campus Revivals. Also Full Gospel Businessmen's Fellowship International and Jews For Jesus – both of which remain active today.**

Some of the more notable and influential figures of these movements are here noted.

# DAVID J. DU PLESSIS

The Charismatic movement was greatly influenced by this early proponent who had been saved under the auspices of black Christians in Africa. Later in South Africa, he became a recognized leader in the Apostolic Faith Mission.

In 1936 during his tenure as executive secretary of the Pentecostal World Conference – a dramatic prophecy was spoken over him by Smith Wigglesworth – David du Plessis was to go "to the uttermost parts of the earth, where God would instigate a Holy Ghost revival in old line denominations."

For more than 35 years David did just that. His book "**The Spirit Made Me Go**" – chronicles his amazing calling and ministry.

# KATHRYN KUHLMAN

One unforgettable itinerant evangelist captured many an audience with her dedication and total dependence on the Holy Spirit, about whom she often preached. **Her name was Kathryn Kuhlman.** This soft-spoken woman of God preached healing before thousands – mantled with the Spirit's power.

From 1947 until her death in 1976 – Kathryn Kuhlman followed the clear mandate of Jesus – *"Greater things than these shall you do..."* She preached about the Holy Spirit and His empowerment to heal the sick, restore sight to the blind, raise the dead and empower the believer.

Speaking of the relevance of the Holy Spirit today she said: "Every church should be experiencing the miracles of Pentecost. Every church should be seeing the healings of the Book of Acts. The gift is for all of us."

The fruit of Kathryn Kuhlman's ministry was ample and powerful. Moreover she strongly influenced many preachers – some of whom are still living and walking in her mantle.

# ORAL ROBERTS

A former Pentecostal Holiness preacher, **Oral Roberts** began his independent deliverance ministry in 1947. He published the Healing Waters Magazine, which by 1953 had a circulation of 265,000. He successfully held huge tent meetings. Oral Roberts reportedly had a "commanding power over demons, over disease and over sin."

The Oral Roberts University he founded in Tulsa, Oklahoma still draws and graduates many thousands of students. Oral Roberts served God faithfully well into his 90's.

In a moving ceremony of impartation – Oral passed on his gift of healing to his son **Richard** who is following in his footsteps, along with his wife Lindsay. They also have a vital television ministry. **Passionately loving the Master to the end – Oral Roberts went to be with his Lord in 2010.**

# OTHER FORERUNNERS OF HEALING EVANGELISM

**William Branham** claimed an awesome angelic visitation prompted his healing revivals. His postwar meetings thereafter became well-known – with documented healings that affected many thousands in many states.

**A. A. Allen** pastored an Assembly of God church in Texas before he too launched revival meetings where the miraculous was much in evidence including (reportedly) the dead being raised!

**Gordon Lindsay** became widely known as a coordinator and actively led the Healing revival. His magazine **The Voice of Healing** greatly assisted the movement.

Healing evangelist **T. L. Osborn's** independent ministry was replete with sensational healings and miracles.

Ordained by the Assemblies of God, **Jack Coe** also witnessed healings in his revival meetings – after being healed himself while in the military in the Second World War.

## HAVEN'T WE OUTGROWN HIM?

**Prevalent for a brief time the "God is dead" philosophy was promoted by infiltrating liberal humanists – who tried to bury GOD in an attempt to remove Him from the culture.**

**Imagine the inconceivable impudence of earthbound creatures – trying to eliminate the Creator upon whom they depend for very breath!**

Obviously these pawns of Satan didn't succeed in erasing God from the fabric of history. And the previous Twentieth Century records of salvation and miraculous deeds – proved over and over that **our GOD – the God of Abraham, Isaac and Jacob – is alive and well!**

## TECHNOLOGY TAKES THE STAGE

**The mind of God – "who knows the end from the beginning" – underscored in Holy Scripture our latter day "increase in knowledge." With the phenomenal inventions of radio, computer technology and television – the soul-saving, life-changing message of Jesus Christ can now be beamed into every corner of the globe.**

# TELEVANGELISTS BREAK
# NEW GROUND

Advancing this new medium, are the following two special emissaries of the Kingdom who were commissioned and empowered. The first of these heralds of hope – was

**PAT ROBERTSON**

A seminary graduate from New York – Pat had the privilege of introducing **Christian Television** to the world!

**Sunday, October 1, 1961** was a "day of small beginnings" when Pat Robertson launched **The 700 Club on WYEH-TV** in Tidewater, Virginia – where he had moved with his wife Dede and 3 children. It was a 'mustard seed' miracle. From that tiny fledgling "prayer and praise" station – the Lord multiplied ministries nationally and around the world with its International Communication Center.

**In 1978 Operation Blessing** began its fleet of trucks carrying relief and humanitarian aid to stricken people and places at home and abroad. **The Flying Hospital** with its surgeons and medical supplies followed.

**In 1982 Mid-East Television** began beaming the Gospel to the Holy Land and surrounding Arab countries. Pat's enduring love for Israel, was instilled in him by his mother in early childhood.

**In 1974** his active engagement with Israel began and continues with his annual highlights of the Feasts (God's Holy Convocations) his prayers for Israel, and news from and about Israel and numerous trips to Israel.

**Pat recently received the Nehemiah Award for his loyalty from Michael Hedding president of the International Christian Embassy in Jerusalem.** Pat is also founder of the Christian Coalition and the American Center for Law and Justice. He is founder and chancellor of Regent University.

**GORDON ROBERTSON** has joined his father in this ongoing multifaceted ministry. Today in its 50th year of broadcasting, the 700 Club World-reach has a global constituency. It is produced in 90 languages in 227 countries and territories. Hundreds of thousands of people have received salvation – including 30 million Soviets.

**Billy Graham commended CBN founder Pat Robertson on his many accomplishments, saying: "Your vision is thrilling." Pat takes no credit.**

**"God gave me a mandate to take the Gospel to the nations. He put CBN here for such a time as this. If He says do it – do it!" Hosting the daily TV program (also on the Internet) at 80 years old – Pat still believes anything is possible!**

"The Lord's getting ready to come back to earth. We say with those in the early church – *the Spirit and the Bride say come. Even so come Lord Jesus.*"

Dr. Robertson's best-selling books include: The End of the Age, The Turning Tide, The New World Order, The Ten Offenses, The New Millennium, Miracles Can Be Yours Today and The Secret Kingdom.

# JOHN HAGEE

**Another seasoned saint and avid promoter of Jesus (Yeshua) and the Holy Land from which He emerged – John Hagee is founding pastor of the huge Cornerstone Church in San Antonio.**

**John Hagee Ministries** is televised daily and there is a weekly radio program. Pastor Hagee is founder and national chairman of **Christians United For Israel (CUFI).** A strong defender of Israel, he hosts an annual spectacular – **"Night To Honor Israel"** during which generous financial support is given to worthy Jewish ministries.

**MATTHEW HAGEE** also a pastor, often shares the pulpit with his father in ministry.

A prolific writer, Dr. Hagee's books include: Beginning of the End, Day of Deception, Final Dawn Over Jerusalem, Jerusalem Countdown, His Glory Revealed and his book – Can America Survive?

**Unfortunately, it is not possible to chronicle here the many other effectual television ministries reaching untold millions with the saving, healing and transforming Gospel of Jesus Christ.**

# THE ULTIMATE LEGACY

The exemplary lives of past and present speakers for God and His Kingdom here narrated – are far more than a catalog of dynamic super-charged personalities successfully impacting a lost humanity with God's promise of *"a hope and a future."*

Rather, they compose a storied progression of the **Almighty God of the Universe** – breathing (through them) upon His precious children – never for a moment relinquishing them to the killing devices of Satan.

**God moved! God touched! God saved! God healed!**

**God used and still uses – the earthen vessels of men and women consecrated to His purpose. The results are astounding.**

**EVANGELISTS IN THE MAKING**

 **DO YOU HEAR THEIR ECHOES?**

Having run their own course – these stalwarts of The Faith continue to encourage generations following. And those who yet proclaim the Gospel – together with those gone before – perpetuate the same truth. **Allow God to have full reign in your life and ministry. The stakes are high! Eternal souls!**

Vested with the mandate of the Master the early disciples of Jesus ran with the vision. They literally turned the world upside down! **GO THOU AND DO LIKEWISE!**

**The 21$^{st}$ century is advancing at an amazing speed!**

**We must work while it is day!**

## TORCHBEARERS OF THE LORD

What structural underpinning will you take with you into **the Father's field?** Spiritual harvesters need wisdom and knowledge and the power of the engrafted Word to "bring them in." Get that *"coal from off the altar"* to touch your lips.

**We are still in the era of the "Latter Rain." The Lord is still saying: *"Whosoever will may come."* And the fire of God empowerment is still available for the asking, seeking, knocking servant.**

# SECTION 3

# Preparing the Ground for Harvest

# SPIRITUAL CLIMATES

**Alter the climate, cleanse the atmosphere and pull down the strongholds**

**In his landmark book Power Shifters – author MICHAEL PITTS,** draws attention to the underlying spiritual component at work in our culture. Though somewhat unfamiliar, the concept he puts forth is certainly worthy of serious consideration.

Citing the histories of various American cities, Pastor Pitts substantiates his findings with solid evidence briefly distilled here.

**Take Las Vegas for example.** This desert hub of erstwhile organized crime made palatable for the public – is the vacation choice of millions who make the trek from around the world. They come to its sophisticated gambling dens propelled by the hope (for so many a false hope) of winning a lot of easy money.

A similar mindset holds the drug addict captive to the promise of that ever elusive "high." Does a specter exist that dominates Las Vegas, with its glitzy hotels, famous Strip and the neon-lit excitement of the Casinos? And is that specter luring its human prey to return again and again? Is this seemingly illogical phenomenon a **"spiritual motivation"** as Pastor Pitts suggests? It bears investigating.

Consider key cities like **New York** the seat of finance, **Washington** the pinnacle of government and power, and **Detroit** with its prevailing auto industry. Each one undeniably has its own particular atmosphere or climate.

Satan often has a hand in this identifying influence. The god of this world with his legions of fallen angels, seeks to manifest in mankind his anti-God agenda. How does he penetrate? **WE OPEN**

**THE DOOR!** Spirits operate in the human mind and heart, where they manipulate and shape the culture with demonic power.

An experienced and thoughtful pastor, Michael Pitts shares his sharply honed insight with conviction. "Spiritual influence creates atmosphere. Atmosphere sustained creates climate. Climate sustained creates strongholds. And strongholds sustained determine culture."

Faced with these subversive maneuverings – do we have to passively yield to the enemy's takeover? Must we be victimized by his sly suggestions? **NO!** Our Creator gave us free will. His Word urges us to stand against the wiles of the devil. *"Resist the devil and he will flee from you."* **THE KEY WORD IS RESIST!**

**How then do we counteract demonic activity? By exercising the voice of faith. By 'suiting up' in the whole armor of God. By engaging in determined spiritual warfare. And by holding fast!**

**According to Michael Pitts – we THE CHURCH are divinely called to be a "counter culture."** We are to shine the brilliant probe of His light in the darkness around us. Satan has no bill of rights, no title deed to God's creation.

Remember Joshua and his armies went to the fortified city of Jericho and marched with blaring trumpets around its walls! They marched over and over – seven times in fact – with confidence in God to give them the victory!

As the divinely called "opposition" we are doing battle today in the enemy's camp. On his turf! **And make no mistake for the "counterculturist" it will be a constant battle!**

The devil's arsenal of combatants against us are: Hatred, cursing and chaos, lying, cheating and the whole sordid gamut of evil. They must be replaced with truth and blessing and the goodness that is God. We must refute and revoke, repress and overpower all

121

the works of the enemy!

**Far better that we be lined up with the WORD OF GOD, that we are 'spiritually correct' in God's estimation – than to be (in the language of our deviant society) politically correct. JESUS – enthroned in us – will alter the climate, cleanse the atmosphere and pull down the strongholds – for His people wherever we are.**

In his well-studied premise, Michael Pitts demonstrates a rare reasoning. Certainly it would be beneficial to anyone wishing to significantly impact a particular place with the Gospel message – to be familiar with the underlying "atmosphere, climate and possible stronghold" of that culture.

We might add yet another "evidence" of spiritual forces at work in other cities such as Pastor Pitts mentions. For instance Ashtabula and its surrounding environs.

# ASHTABULA

### ANOTHER 'EXAMPLE' CITY

**Ashtabula County is the largest in Ohio. Ashtabula City is considered by many to be a stronghold of negativity – of limitation thinking.**

What triggered this city's depressing spiritual climate? The origin of its permeating melancholy may date back to the horrendous Ashtabula train wreck of 1876 – a disaster of unforgettable magnitude.

**December 29th, 1876 was recorded in history as a truly "black Friday."**

With the New Year's Eve celebration just ahead – anxious waiting passengers crowded the railroad station. Their holiday joy was being siphoned by the minute, as an intense winter blizzard pounded the town depositing 20 inches of snow. Icy winds registered 50 miles an hour.

The No. 5 "Pacific Express" train out of Erie, Pennsylvania was already hours late. Eleven coaches drawn by 2 heavy locomotives carried more than 150 souls. An exact list of passengers is not known.

Suddenly, without warning – amid agonizing screams and cries – the train broke through the iron bridge spanning the Ashtabula River and plunged into the chasm of the gulf – 70 foot deep. The enormity of the ensuing fires and carnage was indescribable. A reported 92 passengers and crew were killed and 63 wounded.

Railroad magnate Cornelius Vanderilt later died from shock. Bridge designer and railroad mogul Amassa B. Stone committed suicide.

123

Miraculously, Daniel McGuire, engineer of the first locomotive (the Socrates) had managed to speed his engine over the trestle bridge just before its collapse.

In the overwhelming aftermath repercussions were immediate. However, results of the prior bridge inspections (4 a year), detailed investigations and subsequent verdicts remained controversial.

**The tragic loss of human life on that fatal night shocked the community into a state of perpetual mourning. Much later memorials were installed everywhere – even an audio memorial placed in front of the Hospital that vividly recounts the horrors of the Ashtabula Train Disaster.**

**Philip Paul Bliss and his wife were among those whose remains were never identified. The famous American composer, gospel singer and prolific hymn writer – was also a teacher and full time evangelis**t.

Philip's songs still stir the hearts of Christians and nonbelievers today. Of the hundreds he wrote, these well-known hymns include:

Dare To Be A Daniel

Hallelujah, What a Saviour!

Let the Lower Lights be Burning

Wonderful Words of Life

It is Well With My Soul

Hold the Fort

Jesus Loves Even Me

Almost Persuaded

Later, inside his trunk they found (among many other hymn-poems), the lyrics of Philip's last song written before his death, **"I Will Sing of My Redeemer."** Ironically, that now world-famous song began with these words: **"I know not what awaits me, God kindly veils my eyes…"**

A grief-stricken nation brokenly, but eloquently, mourned his passing along with his beloved wife. Philip Bliss was only 38 years old at his "home-going." A tall obelisk monument stands in Chestnut Grove Cemetery memorializing him and other unrecognizable dead.

**The catastrophic Ashtabula Train Wreck of 1876 – is a story that never ends. Ashtabula still seems to be perpetuating a mindset of fatalism – a "this is the way it is" mentality – toxic thinking.**

To illustrate – reportedly, a good thing happens in Ashtabula and a bad thing is sure to follow. A large mall is built with lots of potential. Then a major company employing hundreds opts to move elsewhere. Mall stores, once popular – head for greener pastures, leaving silent stalls and lost revenues.

A seesaw economy fosters a foreboding sense of uncertainty in the population. Area youth lack initiative and purpose and become embroiled in harmful, often deadly pursuits.

**A phantom of depression envelops the city (and county) – a lingering pall. It may well be a hindering spirit, like the biblical Prince of Persia, Iran – that delayed the answer to Daniel's prayer.** Daniel 10: 13. **Real progress and prosperity is strangely suppressed. It's almost like God went down into the gorge with the train. He didn't!**

**Area churches** are making a valiant effort to lift this county from its "stronghold" of spiritual doldrums – to infuse the life and love of God into its collective being – to put its arms around one individual at a time. More power is needed! ***"Greater is He that is in us than he that is in the world."***

**THE WORD OF GOD is a medicine chest of antidotes to the devil's poisons.** Satan is a master of deceit. He ropes and ties his victims with cords of pleasure and logic and lies. Satan promises freedom from 'righteous restrictions' – but his ultimate agenda is enslavement.

**It is the job of we the called – we the anointed – we the commissioned – to break the yoke – to sever the devil's bonds of imprisonment.**

---

# LOOKING BACK
# LOOKING FORWARD

**In our 21ˢᵗ Century culture there is regrettably a 'reject and abandon' mindset. Ousting God from the mainstream is becoming a commonplace practice. Especially with the advent of the deviously initiated – tolerantly intolerant "political correctness!"**

Blatant departures from Constitutional rights and traditional values have paved the way for a "pick your own god and don't criticize (even slightly) anyone else's" icon. **Unless that is – you're a Christian! And then it seems that nowadays you're fair game for the growing list of activist Christian-bashers!**

Life today is getting more and more difficult. Even law-protected privacy is fast disappearing. Government intrusion is overstepping boundaries at every turn. Godly precepts are getting trampled. It's getting darker.

**We have been called of God to resist! We are to be world-changers! Submissive assimilation into an anti-God environment is not an option! We are commanded to be a counter-culture. We are the Lord's lighthouse and we've been given a purifying light to shine!**

### SOUL WINNERS OF TODAY GIVE HEED.

Before you stand in the presence of those men and women, boys and girls – whom God calls "precious fruit" – do your homework!

**Realize you are preaching THE KINGDOM! A dramatic and permanent change of authority. A Kingdom of righteousness and peace. The Kingdom of our Lord and of His Christ! A glorious Kingdom!**

Engrave on the tablets of your spirit this unalterable truth – **JESUS IS THE KING OF THE KINGDOM!** His Hebrew name *"Yeshua"* means "God save" or "Salvation." *"And the government shall be upon His shoulder and of His kingdom there shall be no end."*

**The good news of salvation comes through the preacher. But the salvation message is not wrapped up in the preacher. First and foremost we *"preach Christ and Him crucified."***

**The dynamic of the Word – the Word that the Almighty dictated – the Word that men gave their lives to make available to everyone – that Word is alive and powerful and eternal!**

**And when it is proclaimed with a fervent anointing – the Lord Himself will show up to vindicate His Word!**

How do we lead the wandering ones to faith in Christ? Through love. Through compassion. Through truth. *"For God did not send His Son into the world to condemn the world, but that the world through Him might be saved."* John 3: 17

Because we ourselves have stood in the place of impending judgment – "there but for the grace of God go I" – we can and we must show compassion. We can and we must love, with the love of the Lord. We can and we must in the strength of our own purified lives – declare His truth – the truth that will "bring them in from the fields of sin."

**When we clothe ourselves in the garments of humility and the white-hot power of the Holy Spirit – when we stand solely in the shadow of the cross – the people will look upon us and – THEY WILL SEE JESUS!**

Inherent in the Gospel is the ability, authority and willingness of Jesus Christ to:

Save completely.

Sanctify wholly.

Break the yoke of satanic bondage.

Reverse the destination of Hell.

Heal body, soul and spirit.

Bestow an abiding peace.

Appoint angelic protection.

Create within us a new DNA

By the Holy Spirit.

Declare us His family.

Give us purpose.

Make us overcomers.

Grant eternal life.

# EVANGELISM THE CALL

## WHAT IS EVANGELISM?

**The late John Wimber,** founder and former International Director of the Association of Vineyard Churches – defined 'evangelism' in the following manner.

"Evangelism is the proclamation of the Kingdom of God in the fullness of its blessing and promise." He further stated: "Evangelism in the power of the Spirit is an essential and integral part of the Kingdom of God, now breaking into the kingdoms of this world, but yet to be consummated at the coming of the King."

"Power evangelism is that gospel presentation which is both rational and transcends the rational; it comes with the demonstration of the power of God, with signs and wonders and introduces the numinous (supernatural guiding force) of God."

## HOW DO WE DEFINE "THE KINGDOM?"

Described in one Bible Dictionary – "the Kingdom of God (or Kingdom of Heaven used interchangeably) refers to when and where God rules, both present and future. A kingdom is a territory ruled over by a king." Gen. 10: 10, Mark 1:15; Matt. 6: 10;

Rev. 12: 10.

## EVANGELISM ACCORDING TO JESUS

**Jesus was the first evangelist.** His methods are

applicable to every time period. When Jesus sent forth His disciples He vested them with His authority. They were given the power to heal, to cast out devils, to preach and teach and baptize and to raise the dead.

*"As the Father has sent Me, I also send you."* **John 20: 21**

The mandate is the same today. **We too have been sent!** In the overcoming power of the Name of Jesus we have the same authority. *"...because as He is , so are we in this world."* 1 John 4: 17

## JESUS CHRIST IS THE SAME – YESTERDAY, TODAY AND FOREVER!

**In His fervent prayer for His disciples – Jesus also prayed for those who believe on His name through their word. What an awesome thought! Jesus Himself prayed for us! John 17: 20**

## THRUST IN THE SICKLE

Whether it is preaching to countless millions in a foreign country or openly sharing the Gospel with the neighbor next door – or preaching the ongoing proclamation of His love to the grocer down the street – evangelism is still the most noble of callings.

Yesterday's 'storm troopers' of evangelism are admittedly a hard act to follow. They went before us – those dedicated "Christ-ones" who carried the vision of hell before their eyes and didn't want anyone to go there! And they passed to us the torch of the Lord.

**Today's voices for God** can learn much of value from our predecessors. But we must take care that as we strive for "pinnacles of success" – we don't overlook the small hills – the little victories. Always remember – the angels rejoice over one soul!

**In our day, in our time – the campaign trail is a wide one extending all around the world. No city is too large. No village is too small. And *"the fields are white with the harvest."***

The winds of latter-day end-times prophecy are rapidly reaching hurricane status. The "day" for working in the vineyard is fast winding up. The night is nearly upon us.

Today's hue and cry of the politically correct and spiritually bank-rupt – our "I'll do it my way" culture – is without doubt a rising devilish crescendo. Now, more than at any other period in history, **the voices of evangelism** must be louder, more insistent and more compelling.

Though the platform of evangelism today has expanded to include radio, TV, the media, publishing and the Internet – the old-fash-ioned tent meeting still thrives. Embrace them all.

We are called to see the world as God views it. We are all God's children by creation. As evangelists we must call them to be His children by redemption. The highways and byways are waiting.

**To you – aspiring evangelists** – you are *"surrounded by a great cloud of witnesses."* Regard them as your cheering section. As you prepare to take **your** place on this present stage of history – fully pack your spiritual suitcase and keep it beside you always.

# ABSOLUTE ESSENTIALS

**THE HOLY SPIRIT** – the first and most important requirement. Skillful homeneutics and compelling stage presence notwithstanding, without the convicting power of the Holy Spirit you may be merely an ineffective lecturer.

**THE SWORD OF THE SPIRIT** – The Word of God!

**KNOWLEDGE** – Knowledge of God; Knowledge of people; Knowledge of Politics and Knowledge of the times.

**A SINGLE HEART** and a focused mindset.

**A PURE CONSCIENCE.**

**BEDROCK BELIEF** and confidence in the One sending you forth.

**A "HOTLINE TO HEAVEN"** – prevailing prayer.

**THE WATER AND BREAD OF LIFE – JESUS CHRIST!**

**EVANGELIST** – Always keep your keys with you – the keys of Commitment and Compassion and Commission. Realize that the world is groaning beneath the weight of its sins and problems and emptiness. Realize afresh that you have the answer!

Trust! Know that as the Lord guides you He provides for you. Know that as the Lord directs you He protects you. The hour is urgent. The harvest is waiting.

*"THY KINGDOM COME! THY WILL BE DONE!*

*ON EARTH AS IT IS IN HEAVEN!"*

It will be worth it all! A day is coming when we shall stand in the presence of GOD and behold the fruit of our labor – souls rescued, souls redeemed, souls transformed – now citizens of Heaven – singing and shouting along with us – VICTORY IN JESUS!

NOW GO!

## POINTERS TO PONDER

1. With earnest prayer and consecration – confirm the call of God upon your life.

2. Carefully consider all the aspects of Power Evangelism especially those the Lord quickens to your heart.

3. Keep a journal of divine impressions and the dates. Refer to it often.

4. Describe the attributes of an evangelist and pinpoint those presently resident in you.

5. Fully identify characteristics lacking in yourself and outline ways to acquire them.

7. When possible discuss these with a pastor or advisor.

8. Heeding the voice of the Spirit draw a roadmap of people and places you are motivated to "evangelize." Incorporate actual maps for ready reference.

9. Do an in-depth study on the individuals, places and people-groups you desire to influence for the Kingdom.

10. Prepare a possible timeline for your outreach.

11. Place pictures before you of people living in another country

and preach Jesus to them. Keep changing the pictures.

12. Do an extensive biographical search of evangelists (past and present) whose ministries especially interest you. Identify why.

12.  Select a particular year in history. Revisit that year. Chronicle on paper its major events, bad and good. Describe how you would reach the people living then with the voice of evangelism and transforming love of Jesus.

# A FINAL WORD

**A mantle of prayer and preparation**

**and the ultimate seal of the Holy Spirit**

**are absolutely incumbent on**

**every soul winner who would**

**say to the God of his own salvation**

**"HERE AM I LORD SEND ME!"**

# SECTION 4
# Study Notes

# A STUDY ON COMPASSION

**Purpose: Getting people not only "feeling" but "doing."**

There is a difference between feeling sorry for someone and having compassion.

Compassion-To be moved, to yearn, to suffer with another, to be affected similarly, to have mercy or show kindness by helping.

Webster says compassion = A strong concern for or sharing in another's suffering but stresses strongly the desire to aid and comfort.

Feeling sorry is a feeling, but compassion always demands a response.

Compassion always moves beyond a feeling and tries to meet a need.

## Examples of compassion in the Word

**The Good Samaritan-** Luke 10:30-37 The Good Samaritan doesn't

just feel sorry for the man on the road, but meets his need.

**Jesus-** Matthew 9:36 "When he saw the crowds, he felt sorry for them. They were confused and helpless, like sheep without a shepherd.

**Jesus-** Matthew 14:14 "When Jesus got out of the boat, he saw the large crowd he felt compassion for them and healed everyone who was sick."

**Jesus-**Matthew 15:32 "Jesus called his disciples together and told them, I feel sorry for these people. They have been with me three days, and they don't have anything to eat. I don't want to send them away hungry. They might faint on their way home."

**Jesus**-Matthew 20:34 "Jesus felt compassion for them and touched their eyes right away they could see, and they became his followers."

**Jesus**- Mark 1:41 "Jesus felt compassion for the man. So he put his hand on him and said I want to now you are well. At once the mans leprosy disappeared and he was well."

Not only did Jesus have pity on people but he had true compassion that moved him to respond.

**Many people feel sorry for this crazy mixed up world, but never allow true compassion to move them out of a feeling and into a solution.**

Although you cannot change the whole world or meet every need if change just one person you have changed the world.

What else does the Bible say: **Matthew 25:31-46; James 2:15-17; John 11:35**

**Questions to think about:**

Do you just feel bad about the this world or do you try to make a difference?

Do you look for needs and try to fill them?

What is the difference between pity and compassion?

What can you do this week to encourage compassion in your circle of influence?

# A STUDY ON PURPOSE AND DESTINY

### Purpose: To teach people about God's purpose and plan for their lives

Matthew 4:18-22 "While Jesus was walking along the shore of Lake Galilee, he saw two brothers. One was Simon, also known as Peter, and the other was Andrew. They were fisherman, and they were casting their nets into the lake. Jesus said to them, "Come with me! I will teach you how to bring in people instead of fish." Right then the two brothers dropped their nets and went with him. Jesus walked on until he saw James and John, the sons of Zebedee. They were in a boat with their father, mending their nets. Jesus asked them to come with him too. Right away they left the boat and their father and went with Jesus. (Contemporary English Version)

*These four disciples had a date with destiny. They were willing to leave everything and follow Jesus. They left their security, families, and jobs to follow a stranger. Why? Because they had a face to face encounter with Jesus their destiny.

Jesus is still walking the roads of life looking for people to follow Him and face their destiny.

You must pursue the call of God! The disciples did not just say they were called they followed Jesus! (Matthew 4:20,22)

Jeremiah 1:4-5 "The Lord said: "Jeremiah, I am your Creator, and before you were born, I chose you to speak for me to the nations." I replied, "I am not a good speaker, Lord, and I am to young."

- You are special to God

- You have unlimited potential

- God has a special plan only you can fulfill

- God doesn't want a clone-be yourself

- God loves you with everlasting love

### How to Discover your Destiny

**"I will bless you with a future filled with hope-a future of success, not of suffering." Jeremiah 29:11**

**1.God's plans are bigger than yours**

- No destiny can be done in yourself

- Who God calls he equips

Excuses

Moses said  – "Use Aaron, I stutter"

Gideon said- "I am little, smallest in my family"

Jeremiah said- "I am to young"

**\*Maybe he called a stutterer, a little one, and young person because the would rely on Him...**

**2. God's plans for you to prosper**

- Why does God want you blessed? So you can bless others!

- It's hard to help others when you are consumed with worry.

**3. God has an inconceivable future for you**

- He has already been in your future to prepare it for you

- God has seen your past to your future

- Why do people not enter the future God has for them? They are scared to give God their dreams. "Will God send me Africa and make me eat monkey meat and fish guts?"

## 4. Desire

**Psalms 37:4 "Do what the Lord wants and he will give you your hearts desire." (C.E.V)**

Delight – Rely on Him for all peace, encouragement, security, Joy

- God always gives you a desire for His will for your life

- Depending on Jesus makes us one in heart, so my desires have naturally and freely lined up with His own.

- God literally places His desire into your heart.

- What are you desires?

- What is your passion?

- What gets you all excited?

Satan tries to kill Destiny

## How?

## 1) Satan tries to attack you spiritually!

- You must lift up a standard against Him!

**Standard – Put to flight, a flag, banner, standard of a larger kind, carried about the army, which may be seen a far off glistening and waving in the air.**

- You are not going under but over!

- If Satan can get you depressed he has already won! You can not fight for others when you are focused on self!

## 2) Temptation

Look at Joseph:

**Potiphar's wife grabbed hold of his coat and said, "Come lay with me!" Joseph ran out of the house, leaving her hanging onto his coat. Genesis 39:12**

Notice that Potiphar's wife did not say I want to destroy your dream so you will lose everything so come sleep with me. No, she was tricky. Satan is also sneaky with how he brings temptation to kill or delay destiny.

## 3) Excuses

Caleb was old Numbers 13:30

Jeremiah was to young Jeremiah 1:4

Joshua was afraid and lacked courage Joshua 1:1-5

Isaiah was sinful Isaiah 6:

Moses was unqualified Exodus 4:10

**\*God never calls the qualified he qualifies the called**

**Questions to think about:**

Are you pursuing God's destiny for your life?

What does God want to do with my life?

Am I trying to be clone of another person or be myself?

Do I offer excuses to God to why I cannot fulfill His plan for my life?

What is my desire could this be God's plan also?

What are other ways that Satan tries to kill destiny?

# A STUDY ON BEING DOWN
## BUT NOT DONE

**Purpose: To teach people not to be weary in well doing**

**"Don't get tired of helping others. You will be rewarded when the time is right, if you don't give up." Galatians 6:9 (C.E.V)**

Weary = Tired

Weary – Worn out, fatigued, tired, having one's patience; pleasure or interest worn out.

Greek says it this way: Desperate, faint, labor, toil, to be beaten down.

Faint – To unloose, as a bow string, to relax, to lack courage, to lose heart, to grow weary or tired.

Today many people start out all fired up but soon lose heart they become beaten down and tired they even quit!

Satan hits us with his fiery darts every day to cause us to grow tired in doing well.

**"Let your faith be like a shield, and you will be able to stop all the flaming arrows of the evil one." Ephesians 6: 16 (C.E.V)**

**"Finally, let the mighty strength of the Lord make you strong, so defend yourself against the devil's tricks. We are not fighting against forces and authorities and against rulers of darkness and powers in the spiritual world. So put on all the armor that God gives. Then when that evil day comes, you will be able to defend yourself. And when the battle is over, you will still be standing firm." Ephesians 6: 10-17**

Are you putting on your armor every day?

Your armor will help you defend yourself against the battle of weariness.

### 3 area's that Satan cause us to grow tired in doing well

**1)Righteous and Holy Living**

Daniel 3: 16 **"The three men replied, 'Your majesty, we don't need to defend ourselves. The God we worship can save us from**

**you and the flaming furnace. <u>But even if he doesn't, we still won't worship your gods and the golden statue you have set up.</u>"**

Shadrach, Meshach, and Abednego refused to bow to this world. They stood up for righteousness and holy living will you?

**2) Devotion time with God**

Mark 1:35: **"Very early in the morning, while it was still dark, Jesus got up, left the house and went off to a solitary place, where he prayed."**

Luke 5:16: **"But Jesus often withdrew to lonely places and prayed."**

Luke 6:12: **"...Jesus went into the hills, and spent the night praying to God."**

**<u>"If you have some time on your hands, spend part of it on your knees."– Corrie Ten Boom</u>**

Romans 8:26; Matthew 7:7-8; Psalms 86:5-7; 1 Peter 4:7; Psalms 66:20; Matthew 5:43-45a; 2 Chronicles 7:14; Matthew 21:22; Acts 2:42; Philippians 4:6; Revelation 5:8; Matthew 5:44; Matthew 6:8; James 5:16b; Romans 12:12

Do not allow Satan steal your prayer life. He often whispers in the ear of the believer that you're wasting your time so give up! Do not grow Weary! No time spent in His presence is wasted time but invested time!

**3) Sharing your faith**

Mark 16:15: **"Go and preach the good news to everyone in the world."**

Acts 4: 18-20: **So they called the two apostles back in and told them that they must never, for any reason, teach anything about the name of Jesus. Peter and John answered, "Do you think God wants us to obey you or to obey him? We cannot keep quiet about what we have seen and heard."**

*Look how Peter and John reacted when they were ordered not to witness for Christ.

Romans 1:16: **"I am not ashamed of the gospel of Christ: for it is the power of God unto salvation to everyone that believes to the Jews first, and also to the Greek."**

*Why was Paul not embarrassed of the gospel?

**If Satan can get you to grow tired in sharing your faith he has won the world!**

**Beaten men walk beaten paths, but diligent men blaze trails- Willard Beesley**

**Questions to think about:**

Are you tired right now in any of these three areas?

Are you putting on the armor of God?

Are you willing to stand up for your faith rather grow tired in sharing it?

Are you ashamed of sharing the gospel?

What is your prayer life like?

# A STUDY ON OVERCOMING YOUR PAST

**Purpose: Teaching people to have victory over their past so they can blast into their future.**

Philippians 3:10-14: **"All I want is to know Christ and the power that raised him to life. I want to suffer and die as he did, so that somehow I also may be raised to life. I have not yet reached my goal, and I am not perfect. But Christ has taken hold of me. So I keep on running and struggling to take hold of the prize. My friends, I don't feel that I have already arrived. <u>But I forget what is behind, and I struggle for what is ahead.</u> I run toward the goal, so that I can win the prize that God offers because of what Christ Jesus has done."**

**3:10** God wants us to walk in His power not settling for a sub-par Christianity.

- The past can choke His power flowing through us

- Satan's greatest weapon against us is our past.

- He will dig up every past mistake to keep us sad and focused on self not others.

- Satan's goal is to destroy your faith and love for God by using your past.

- We can spend much time by trying to overcome our past

- If your past is not dealt with it can lead to depression

## Five keys to getting free from your past

### 1) Ask God for a fresh discovery of the blood

Hebrews 9: 13-14: **"According to the law of Moses, those people who became unclean are not fit to worship God. Yet they will be considered clean, if they are sprinkled with the blood of goats and bulls and with the ashes of a sacrificed calf. But Christ was sinless, and he offered himself as an eternal and spiritual sacrifice to God. That's why his blood is much more powerful and makes our consciences clear. Now we can serve the living God and no longer do things that lead to death." (C.E.V.)**

- The blood when applied to your heart will bury your past forever and no longer will be remembered in Heaven.

- To dwell on our past is to insult God.

- When you say, My sin is to **BIG** for God to forgive" you are telling God that His blood was not good enough. This of course is crazy!

Romans 3:25-26: **"God sent Christ to be our sacrifice. Christ offered his life's blood, so that by faith in him we could come to God. And God did this to show that in the past he was right to be patient and forgive sinners. This also shows that God is right when he accepts people who have faith in Jesus." (C.E.V.)**

Romans 5:9: **"But there is more! Now that God has accepted us because Christ sacrificed his life's blood, we will also be kept safe from God's anger. (C.E.V.)**

Justification = Just as if it never happened

- **In forgiveness we are stripped of the vile and stinking rags of our sins; In justification we are clothed upon the glory of Christ** – R. A. Torrey

- Repentance – <u>Turning away from sin;</u> we are not using forgiveness as a crutch to sin, but agreeing with God that what we have done is wrong

## 2) <u>Forgive yourself</u>

**Micah 7:18-19: "Our God, no one is like you. We are all left of your chosen people, and freely forgive our sin and guilt. You do not stay angry forever; you are glad to have pity and pleased to be merciful. You will trample on our sins and throw them in the sea."**

- When you torment yourself for past sin and refuse to forgive yourself, It is like telling the devil "Do not leave I enjoy having you around."

- To refuse to forgive yourself is to give the devil a foothold in your life.

- Being forgiven does not always liken with feeling forgiven

- God does not keep a video of all your sins, the oldies plus the new releases.

- He tramples on them, smashes them to bits and hurls them into the sea.

- God cannot replay the film because He does not even own them anymore they are destroyed!

- <u>To God, forgiven means forgotten</u>

- When you forgive yourself you allow God to heal the hurt that is hidden deep within your life

- If God feels so strongly about forgetting sin why do you not forgive yourself?

## 3) Forget the past

**"God takes all our sin and throws them in the deepest ocean and puts a big sign that says 'No Fishing'"**

- How can you drive your car when you are looking only through your rear view mirror. How can you move forward in life when you are still looking at yesterday?

- Paul says to Forget the past and move on **(Philippians 3:10-14)**

- You will never grow in God until you let go of the past

- Don't fish up your past leave it in the ocean

## 4) Forgive others who hurt you

Ephesians 4:32: **"Instead, be kind and merciful, and forgive others, just as God forgave you because of Christ."**

Colossians 3:13-14: **"Put up with each other, and forgive anyone who does you wrong, just as Christ has forgiven you. Love is more important than anything else. It is what ties everything completely together."**

**Check out this:**

The parable of the king and the unforgiving servant:

**Matthew 18:23-35**

Joseph's story of forgiveness for his brothers:

**Genesis 45**

Jesus forgives His enemies:

**Luke 23:33-34**

- In Luke 15: 29-30 The elder brother was so angry he could not refer to his brother as brother, because of lack of forgiveness it became an obstacle to the happiness and riches that already belonged to him.

- Are you allowing someone else to rob you from enjoying life?

## 5) <u>Embrace God's forgiveness and let Him set you free</u>!

Embrace = To clasp or hold to one with the arms. To not let go!

- Clasp on to God's forgiveness and never let go

- Making the choice to turn away from sin is the first step toward true freedom

- You have never gone to far for God to forgive you!

- Receive God's full pardon today

**Study: Isaiah 43:58, Jeremiah 31:34, Hebrews 10:15-17,**

**1 John 1:9, Matthew 6:12,14,15, Mark 11:25, Luke 6:37-38, Matthew 18:21, Luke 17:3-5**

**Things to think about:**

Are you freed from your past so you can blast into your destiny?

Do you have unforgiveness for anyone?

Do you forgive yourself when you do wrong or do you ask yourself these questions: "I cannot believe I did that"; "I did that, how could I?"; "I knew better than that"; "My sin is too big for God to forgive!"

**(Romans 8:1)**

# A STUDY ON WHO GOD IS AND WHO HE'S NOT!

**Purpose: To teach people about who is God so they will desire to serve Him.**

Phillipians 2: 10,11 **"So at the name of Jesus everyone will bow down, those in heaven, on earth, and under the earth. And to the glory of God the Father everyone will openly agree, "Jesus Christ is Lord!"**

- Some people will not bow their knee to God because they have a false view of who God is!

- Some people will not tell their friends about God because they also have a false view who God is.

- You will not serve someone you do not know or grasp!

- How do you perceive God to be like?

## Who God is Not

### 1. God is just like my earthly father

- If you have a awesome earthly father this will strengthen your view on God

- If you have had a bad experience with your earthly father this will warp your view on the fathers love

### 2. God is more willing to judge and condemn you than He is to bless you

### 3. God loves to terrorize you

**4.God is a big cosmic kill joy**

**5. God forces people against their will to serve Him**

**6. God is a big auditor in heaven which records all your wrongs and throws them in your face**

**7. God will not forgive you because your sin is to big for Him to forgive**

**Who God is**

**1.God is Love 1 John 4:19** "We love Him because he first loved us." **John 3:16**

**2. God is Light 1 John 1:5** "God is light and in Him is no darkness at all."

**3. God Cares 1 Peter 5:7** "Casting your all cares upon Him; for he cares for you."

**4. God Forgives 1 John 1:9** "If we confess our sins, he is faithful and just to forgive us our sins, and to cleanse us from all unrighteousness"

**5. God Gives Peace** He is the Prince of Peace

**6. God Restores Joel 2:25** "And I will restore to you the years that the locust has eaten."

**7. God is full of mercy and great kindness Joel 2:13** "Don't rip your clothes to show your sorrow. Instead turn back to me with broken hearts for I am gracious and merciful, slow to anger, and great kindness and I don't like to punish."

**Things to think about**

What is your view of God?

Do you compare Him with your earthly father?

Do you allow false perceptions of God to hinder why you evangelize?

# A STUDY ON REVOLUTION

### Purpose: Teaching people to evangelize

What is a hero?

Hero – one who is on fire for God and starts a fire in their circle of influence

In the world of fallen heroes, there needs to be true heroes that stand up for their God and start a revolution!

### Acts 17:6b "Paul and Silas have been upsetting things everywhere. Now they have come here,"

- Paul an Silas were true heroes, they radically changed their world so much that people knew when they were coming!

- What to people say when they see you coming?

### Job Description of a Revolutionary

1) One who can't stand to see the status quo stay the status quo

2) One who stirs things up

3) One who doesn't leave things the same

4) One who not only is on fire but starts a fire

5) One who doesn't just blend in but goes against the flow

### What could happen in a Revolution

1) People hate you

2) Persecution

**Matthew 5:10-12 "God blesses those people who are treated badly for doing right. They belong to the kingdom of heaven. God will bless you <u>when people insult you, mistreat you, and tell all kinds of evil lies about you because of me</u>. Be happy and excited! You will have a great reward in heaven. People did these same things to the prophets who lived long ago."**

3) People get mad at you

4) <u>You could save your whole school or work place from HELL!!</u>

- Give people a chance to choose the right thing even if it means getting people mad

- Before you even get to school or work ask yourself what a revolution would look like

- Yes, some will be offended at you for sharing Jesus, but others will rejoice that they have been saved through your revolution

- It is time we take back our cities, our schools, and our families and let people know there is a Jesus!

- It is time we make it hard for souls to go Hell in our cities!

- Make a legacy right now

## Things to think about

What are some things you can do to let your work/school know a revolution is coming?

What would it look like with thousands coming to your church because of you?

What would the bible clubs at school look like if a revolution hit your school?

What would it look like if thousands of people prayed over their meals?

What would it look like if your principal/boss and teachers/co-workers became saved?

What would it look like if everyone was talking about God rather than cussing and talking dirty?

What would you do if you had a reputation like Paul?

Write down 5 people you want to become saved and bring to church **PRAY FOR THEM!!!!!!!**

1)

2)

3)

4)

5)

**COMMIT TO PRAY FOR THEM EVERY DAY FOR THE**

**NEXT 8 WEEKS**

<u>**Here are some things to pray for:**</u>

1. For soft hearts to hear the gospel

2. For open hears to hear the truth

3. For open eyes to see the light

4. That God would show up in your work/school

5. That your church would grow

6. That a revival would invade your city

**7. For your leaders and workers**

Write your vision of what you would like to see happen in your work/school and all the hang outs as a result of this revolution.

# A Study on Revolution part 2

**Purpose: Teaching people to be fervent in evangelism**

Revolution = **Acts 17:6 "These that have turned the world upside down are coming here also."**

What does it mean to be on fire?

**Fervent = Having or showing great emotion or warmth; Extremely hot; glowing**

**Ignited        =To set on fire; to cause to burn; to arouse the passion of**

**Righteous = good; moral; up right**

**Explosion = a sudden great increase; outburst**

**In other words being on fire is being extremely fervent and hot for God, igniting others with that fire, spreading good news in a powerful manner that brings a sudden increase into the kingdom of God!**

Fire is not a emotion

Fire is not a game

Fire is not a temporary feeling

**Jeremiah 20:9 "His word is in my heart like a fire shut up in my bones. I am weary of holding it indeed I cannot."**

Joshua 1:6-9 **"Long ago I promised the ancestors of Israel that I would give this land to their descendants. So be strong and brave! Be careful to do everything my servant Moses taught you. Never stop reading the book of the law he gave you. Day**

**and night you must think about what it says. If you obey it completely, you and Israel will be able to take this land. I've commanded you to be strong and brave. Don't ever be afraid or discouraged! I am the Lord your God, and I will be there to help you wherever you go."** (C.E.V.)

- Moses is now dead

- Joshua is ready to start a revolution

- Joshua is leading millions of people into a land of giants

- Your work/school can be like a "Land of Giants" but be strong!

- The word gives you courage (V.8)

- God does not ask us to be strong he commands us. (V.9)

- A revolution is not a job for wimps

- A revolution takes back bone

- Now is the time: Today is the day for revolution

- Don't wait until later

- Be a history maker

- God has promised that he would Go with us into the land of giants

- Don't let the devil have your friends

- The very nature of a revolution is going to take somebody who has a F.I.R.E. inside them that could not care less about what others think!

*God will be there for you as you be bold for Him, and tell others, getting the word out, as you stir things up, and refuse to allow and tolerate sin and garbage and perversion in your cities!!!!!

**Things to think about:**

Does your fire make other people feel out in the cold?

Do you think Joshua ever was scared as he looked toward a land full of giants with three million behind him?

What do you think Joshua did when he started feeling a little troubled?

What are some things that you can do this week to make sure people in your work/school and town know about your church?

## Things to think about:

Does your fire make other people feel out in the cold?

Do you think Joshua ever was scared as he looked toward a land full of giants with three million behind him?

What do you think Joshua did when he started feeling a little troubled?

What are some things that you can do this week to make sure people in your work/school and town know about your church?

# A STUDY ON SPIRITUAL WARFARE

**Purpose: teaching people how to defeat their enemy and take back their world!**

Satan has a three-fold plan for your life:

**John 10:10 "A thief (Satan) comes only to rob, kill, and destroy. I come so that everyone would have life, and have it in its fullest."**

<u>Rob</u> from your soul

<u>Kill </u>your body

<u>Destroy</u> your spirit

<u>God also has a plan and that is to give you Life! </u>

In every war there is always a war plan. No one goes into battle blind!

**2 Corinthians 2:11 "Lest Satan should get an advantage of us: for we are not ignorant of his devices."**

Devices = Schemes

• Satan is scheming and planning on how he can take you to Hell and accomplish his 3 fold plan for your life.

**Ephesians 6: 11,12 "Put on all the armor that God gives, so you can defend yourself against the devil's tricks. We are not fighting against humans. We are fighting against forces and authorities and against rulers of darkness and powers in the spiritual world.**

- Satan has an organized military he does not run a sloppy operation.

**2 Timothy 2:26 "They have been trapped by the devil, and he makes them obey him, but God may help them escape."**

- Satan is still setting traps for God's people

**Job 1:10 "You are like a wall protecting not only him, but his entire family and his property. You make him successful in whatever he does, and his flocks and herds are everywhere."**

- There is hedge or a wall protecting us from Satan if we know Christ

**Job 1:12 "The Lord replied, "All right, Satan, do what you want with anything that belongs to him, but don't harm Job. Then Satan left."**

- Satan is limited in his attacks, everything has to go through God

**Genesis 3:1a "The snake (Satan) was sneakier than any of the other wild animals that the Lord God had made."**

- Satan is tricky and sneaky in his attacks

**Revelation 12:10b "Satan accuses our people in the presence of God day and night. Now he has been thrown out!"**

- Satan is the accuser of God's people

**Luke 4:13 "After the devil had finished testing Jesus in every way possible, he left him for a while."**

- When you win a battle the war is not over! Higher levels bigger devils!

## 4) The word of our testimony

• There is power in praise

• Do you tell your testimony to other people?

## 5) Surrender to God

James 4:7 **"Surrender to God! Resist the devil, and he will run from you."**

• Only can one who has surrendered to God, confront the devil and have victory!

• Run = run in terror.

• Satan will run in terror when we surrender to God.

## 6) Use your authority

Luke 10: 18-20 **"Jesus told them: I saw Satan fall from heaven like a flash of lightning. I have given you power to trample on snakes and scorpions and to defeat the power of your enemy Satan. Nothing can harm you. But don't be happy because evil spirits obey you. Be happy that your names are written in heaven!"**

Luke 9:1 **"Jesus called together his twelve apostles and gave them complete power over all demons and diseases.**

• If you are in Christ you have authority over Satan and his kingdom

• Do not get cocky because you have authority, be happy God saved you!

**Things to think about**

Are you ready to fight the Devil if he comes to bother you?

Do you know the Word?

Are you surrendered to God?

We are in a spiritual war will you enlist to invade the darkness?

## More books by Steve Porter

***Crocodile Meat-*** *New and Extended Version*

***Crocodile Meat-*** *Student Version*

***You Shall Not Surely Die-*** *The Dangers of Inhalant Drug Abuse and the CURE through Jesus Christ*

***Invading the Darkness- Power Evangelism Training 101***

***Limitless -*** *7 Values of Highly Successful People*

***Whispers from the Throne Room-*** *Reflections on the Manifest Presence*

**Letters to the Wounded Warrior- God's Loving Message of Healing and Restoration for the Church**

***He Leads Me Beside Still Waters-*** *50 Love Letters of Healing and Restoration from our Lord*

***Facebook Pearls-*** *A Intimate Devotional*

**Draw Me-** The Cry of the Bride **(Coming Soon)**

# www.findrefuge.tv

Contact Info

**Refuge Ministries**

**P.O Box 381**

**Bloomfield, NY 14469**

**www.findrefuge.tv**

**Rescue. Restore. Revive**

Made in the USA
Middletown, DE
17 September 2017